# SECRETS OF SUCCESSFUL SPEAKING

Maureen Hanigan

COLLIER BOOKS
MACMILLAN PUBLISHING COMPANY
NEW YORK
COLLIER MACMILLAN PUBLISHERS
LONDON

Copyright © 1980 by Maureen Wenk Hanigan

All rights reserved. No part of this book may be reproduced or transmitted in any form or by any means, electronic or mechanical, including photocopying, recording or by any information storage and retrieval system, without permission in writing from the Publisher.

Macmillan Publishing Company
866 Third Avenue, New York, N.Y. 10022
Collier Macmillan Canada, Inc.

Library of Congress Cataloging in Publication Data

Hanigan, Maureen Wenk.
Secrets of successful speaking.

Previously published as: Ms., you look great! How do you sound?
1. Oral communication.   2. Women—Communication.
I. Title.
P95.H36   1984      001.54′2      84-11243
ISBN 0-02-012420-1 (pbk.)

Macmillan books are available at special discounts for bulk purchases for sales promotions, premiums, fund-raising, or educational use. Special editions or book excerpts can also be created to specification. For details, contact:

Special Sales Director
Macmillan Publishing Company
866 Third Avenue
New York, New York 10022

First Collier Books Edition 1984

10  9  8  7  6  5  4  3  2  1

Printed in the United States of America

Previously published as *Ms., You Look Great! How Do You Sound?*

THIS BOOK IS DEDICATED

To Tom, who gave my life a reason and a
 greater worth —
To Helenmarie, who gave it beauty, fulfillment
 and a reaffirmation of faith —
To Maurelia, who filled it with adventure,
 sunshine and a lilting grace —
 and
To Marietta, who added laughter and then
 encircled it with love.

# CONTENTS

**INTRODUCTION** x
  Why improving your speech is important

**CHAPTER ONE** 3
  Initial Personal Quiz

**CHAPTER TWO** 7
  A speech class for one — you!
  A physical check-up
  Establishing a basic tone
  How to determine the right pitch for you
  Eliminating any nasal tendency
  Articulation drills

**CHAPTER THREE** 18
  Parties are supposed to be fun; but are they?
    Starting a conversation
    Meeting a celebrity
    Excessive drinkers
    The casanova

**CHAPTER FOUR** 26
  Personal introductions

**CHAPTER FIVE** 29
  Your job interview
    Do your homework
    When you arrive
    Conducting an interview

**CHAPTER SIX** 36
  Tips for the career woman
    Looking toward advancement
    Training others and giving instructions
  The business meeting
    Selling
    When should you speak up?

The business talk
　　　　An "eloquent" business talk
　　　　Show and tell (how to use visual aids)

　**CHAPTER SEVEN**                          53
　　　How do you look on the telephone?
　　　　Why are you shouting?
　　　　Your tape recorder
　　　　Overcoming speech tics
　　　　Telephone manners

　**CHAPTER EIGHT**                            60
　　　Overcoming submissive speech

✓ **CHAPTER NINE**                            64
　　　Don't allow your voice to be older than you are
　　　Careless speech habits

　**CHAPTER TEN**                                71
　　　Being shy is not an excuse
　　　　Social shyness
　　　　Too shy to speak out
　　　　The Sunday service reader

　**CHAPTER ELEVEN**                        77
　　　Introducing a speaker
　　　　How to prepare
　　　　At the podium

✓ **CHAPTER TWELVE**                      81
　　　You too can be a guest speaker
　　　Nerves; you can control them
　　　Prepare yourself
　　　Preparing your speech
　　　　The beginning
　　　　The body
　　　　The end

viii

CHAPTER THIRTEEN     104
    The question period

CHAPTER FOURTEEN     110
    Why you should study Public Speaking if
    you are never going to speak in public

CHAPTER FIFTEEN     114
    Let's look at the way you listen
    Can you identify the caring people in
    a public place?
    How do you rate your listening ability?

CHAPTER SIXTEEN     121
    Suggestions for talking with the hard of hearing

CHAPTER SEVENTEEN     126
    Why a "poker voice" is only good for poker
    Drills to correct a monotone

CHAPTER EIGHTEEN     134
    How to handle an embarrassing mistake

CHAPTER NINETEEN     140
    How to disagree and stay friends
    The Do's and the Don'ts

CHAPTER TWENTY     149
    We'd like to interview you on TV

CHAPTER TWENTY-ONE     154
    Just between us!

# Introduction

## Why Improving Your Speech is Important

Are you really on the move? Are you seriously and conscientiously trying to improve? Do you still feel you need a bit more inner confidence in order to project the image for which you are striving? It may be that you have not yet addressed the one area that will ultimately determine how far you will progress and how quickly you will meet your goals.

If you have invested half of your pay check to have your hair brightened and styled in a most flattering cut — have spent hours practicing how to apply your make-up so that it appears natural — have pored over fashion magazines and studied the most astute ways to strengthen your wardrobe budget — have really established an exercise program with which you can live, and have finally taken off those extra pounds — you're on your way! Don't be defeated now by overlooking the most important assets of all — your voice and your speech! They will enhance or ruthlessly destroy everything you have worked for the very minute you start to talk. Are they really that important? Yes, Ms. — they are.

There is no single factor by which a person is judged more quickly than by her speech. It supercedes appearance. How often have you been attracted to someone by her sense of style, but lost interest almost the minute she started to engage you in a conversation? A person's voice tells so much about her personality, her education, her social and business standing and even her age. It is also often an instant barometer of her health and most important of all, her attitude.

Here are the areas of speech and speech related matters that will be covered in the following pages to give you the greatest amount of profit. Together we shall consider those things most important in establishing you as an effective and competent speaker.

- How you can be sure your voice is both pleasing and commanding
- How to be at ease when it is necessary to speak before a group
- How to be more relaxed and self-assured when talking to others in a business or social situation
- How to handle difficult situations and disagree without arguing
- How to use your voice to project your sincerity, your authority and your convictions clearly and effectively
- How to present yourself at your best in both the business and volunteer world
- How to check on your listening habits and improve them
- How to judge more astutely what is said and what is inferred
- How to introduce a speaker or present a talk of your own
- How to become more aware each day of the image you are establishing by your voice and speech patterns

Now that the doors all the way up to the president's office have finally opened and women in all fields are qualifying to sit behind executive desks, it is crucial that you show your abilities and personality in a most positive and convincing manner.

Perhaps you have observed two women equally well-qualified in the same company, both knowledgeable and well groomed, but one advances and the other seems to remain at the same desk year after year. She may have the intelligence, the experience and the reliability needed for the next level of advancement, but there is always some ambivalence among her superiors when her name is reviewed, and she stays in the same position. What is lacking? Could it be her inability to speak well and present herself in a manner that shows her capabilities? It could be a simple voice or speech problem.

Do you realize that when you speak on the phone with someone whom you have never met, you form a definite mental picture of her by the end of the conversation, no matter how short the time, based solely on her speaking voice? If you later meet the person her appearance may surprise you, but it will not alter the subtle impressions you have already established.

Unfortunately, speech is often a neglected field of grooming; but your speech cosmetics will take precedent over your style cosmetics when it comes to proving your worth to a major business concern. It will most certainly be your greatest asset if your ambitions tend toward establishing your own business, no matter what its nature may be. It will be an unqualified measure of your value to any volunteer group and it will quickly establish your social standing if you move to a new community.

Few people realize that their speech is not an unalterable part of their personality. It can easily be improved and in most cases, especially for those in the work force and seeking advancement, such improvement may be crucial. Women serving on various boards within the community, conducting meetings or raising funds in volunteer groups, or those frequently called upon to introduce professional speakers and representing civic organizations, will do well to check the quality of their voice and their speech patterns. A voice that is well modulated, pleasing to listen to, able to instill confidence, command authority and project sincerity is an enviable asset for every woman. There is one more advantage to a rich, full voice — it is definitely sexier. Consider for a moment the movie stars recognized as the most seductive and recall the tones of their voices. You will never hear an alluring leading lady with a high squeaky pitch.

If you are to be admired, confided in and promoted, you must know what you are about — and you must show it! We are a nation immersed in packaging but before you can sell people your product you must first convince them that you are a worthwhile investment. Few have professional managers; it is up to you to sell your own abilities in the marketplace.

Honestly, have you ever heard anyone being admired because she was indecisive, unsure of herself and disorganized? When has anyone remarked to you, "Isn't she marvelous — she doesn't have any idea what she's doing, and she's so nervous she can't think of her own name." If you know your material thoroughly that's great, but equally important you must know how to present it effectively. There are no Brownie points today (nor have there ever been) for shaking knees and high, tight voices.

Assuming now that you know your job or you are making a sincere effort toward mastering it, this book will show you how to take a giant step. It is also basic that you establish realistic goals and map out both a time table and a plausible program for reaching them. The following pages are not about packaging empty boxes, because no matter how cleverly that is done, window dressing seldom remains around for long.

This book is written for the positive woman who is

looking toward an upward curve, who is willing to make the effort and go the extra mile to achieve her aims. If you are this kind of woman it will show you step by step how to best showcase your abilities, your knowledge, your originality and your positive upbeat personality. (If you don't think you have all of these qualities, you may be selling yourself short and that is the most fatal of all mistakes.)

Start working on your speech and you will find that you will uncover a more confident personality. There is no reason for someone else to present your ideas in a more saleable manner than you present them. You are fully as capable as the next person.

There are related matters to be checked also. Facial expressions, what your hands are saying while you're speaking, posture and nervous habits which have crept into your daily speech are tell-tale signs of apprehension when you begin to address a group. It is still nice to know when you have finished speaking that the applause is for what you said and not because you finally sat down!

Now is not the time to procrastinate about positive self-improvements. The time has come and a different drummer has already started to play, and when you are called upon now, you had best be able to lead the parade. So, let's start to work on some basic techniques to help you convince yourself — and then, show the world!

# SECRETS
# OF
# SUCCESSFUL
# SPEAKING

## Chapter One

### Initial Personal Quiz

You must have a starting point. If you find your weakest area you will know where to begin. Try answering the following questions thoughtfully and with scrupulous honesty. When in doubt, assume the area needs improvement. Since we do not hear ourselves accurately, you might find it helpful to check some of your answers with a family member or a close friend upon whom you can rely to be candid.

1. Have you sometimes been aware of a tendency to speak too loudly or too softly?
2. Do you speak so quickly that you are often asked to repeat?
3. Do you think at times you might have made the same point, just as clearly, with fewer words?
4. Are you aware that you use a cliche such as, "at that point in time", "feedback", "you know", etc.? (Better check this with someone else.)
5. Do you catch yourself interrupting others?
6. Do you place the burden of conversation on others when you are in a group and feel somewhat uncomfortable?
7. Do you have to depend upon a drink to feel relaxed when you meet new people? Is it your source of confidence?
8. Are you apt to slur the endings of your words? Are

Ds, Ns and Ts almost omitted?
9. How often do you say, "What I really mean is . . ." or "The point I'm trying to make is . . ."?
10. Do you tend to monopolize conversations? Does this happen more often when you are tired, nervous or after cocktails?
11. Do waitresses and others not accustomed to your speech patterns ask you to repeat?
12. If you stand about six feet away from a mirror and recite something with which you are familiar, is it obvious that you are using your tongue, lips and jaw as you speak?
13. Do you think it shows sophistication or worldliness to incorporate slang, vulgarities or curses into informal conversations? How about foreign phrases?
14. Do you smile often and find you can relax easily?
15. Do you overdramatize most stories?
16. Do you connect all sentences with "and" or "er"?
17. Do you frequently suffer from laryngitis?
18. When standing for a long period of time do you often find yourself off balance?
19. Are you comfortable with your hands when you're speaking?
20. Do you look directly at the person with whom you are talking?
21. Do you *really* listen?

It is not only discouraging but almost impossible to work intently on numerous weaknesses at the same time and achieve dramatic success. Sometimes, however, you may find that by concentrating on one area the bi-product of that improvement has been the elimination of a related mistake. A happy bonus!

In order to gain maximum help from this book, try following these suggestions.

Begin by reading the book through completely. Mark

passages and weaknesses which you feel particularly apply to your voice or speech patterns.

Go back then and read the first paragraphs which seemed to refer to you personally. Work only on that one area for several weeks. If drills are given you may wish to expand them. You may also find that a trip to the library will furnish valuable additional material once you have pin-pointed the area on which you need to work. You will find entire books devoted to conversational speech as well as to public speaking and others written on voice quality. Any exercise that is beneficial in strengthening the singing voice will also prove helpful in improving the speaking voice.

Don't demand or expect too much of yourself. It is especially easy on a solo project to become discouraged and feel not enough progress is being made. If you are now consciously aware of ending most of your sentences with "you know", or you realize that you are straining your voice or speaking too rapidly, these are the first steps and an excellent start. Realize that it will take some time to change a long established habit so give yourself that time, and also credit for having the fortitude to make the effort to become a more effective speaker. It may be frustrating at first, but at the end of two weeks, you'll find it is only occasionally that you hear yourself slipping back into the old patterns. Now you are ready to move on, perhaps to those articulation drills which show progress more quickly as those crisp clear sounds emerge.

This book was not created for a bookcase. It needs to be on your desk, or night table, or the kitchen shelf — wherever you are most likely to see it and pick it up from time to time; even if it's just to move it or dust under it. Once you have read it and have practiced the drills most important to you, or have made up your mind about the positive attitude you are going to encompass about speaking up or speaking well, just a glance at the cover will remind you about the improvement you want to make.

THIS BOOK WAS BORN TO BE ADOPTED, NOT BOUGHT. You have brought home a friend who wants to help you, and one who asks only a conspicuous place in your home. Do find a place for it, and then watch how well it will serve you and how quickly it will improve your image, reinforce your self-confidence and advance your potential for success.

# Chapter Two

## A Speech Class for One — You!

One of the best loved musicals of all times is "My Fair Lady." Tens of thousands have watched enthralled, as Eliza Doolittle was transformed from a Cockney flower girl into a lady of gentility. Remember the main instrument that accomplishes this dramatic transformation? It is the change in her voice quality and her diction that is the focal point of the entire production. Audiences the world over have struggled in empathy with her as she valiantly tried over and over again to tell us correctly that "the rain in Spain falls mainly on the plains." It was made perfectly clear that her gown could be selected quickly, but precious time must be spent on her speech. It is the moment when she starts to talk that the crucial judgement will come. Her speech will decide who she is! How many in the audience were astute enough to ask themselves if their own voices could be improved to reinforce their abilities? You understood the message, and you realized the importance of a vibrant, arresting voice; that is why you picked up this book. It will not disappoint you.

In this chapter you will take the first basic steps in developing your own natural voice to its fullest potential. You will start with a quick physical check, and once assured that you have no obstructions to producing a clear speech, you will move on to the fundamental exercises which enhance your tones and strengthen them.

You will then have accomplished your first major effort in your own personal quest for recognition and respect for your unique talents.

## Physical Check-Up

In order to produce sounds correctly, all the physical instruments used must be in perfect working order. Try these simple tests and become your own "Speech Mechanic."

Clench your teeth tightly. The back teeth on each side (your molars) should mesh together. Your upper front teeth should close slightly over your lower front teeth. An overshot jaw, or an undershot jaw (when the lower front teeth close over the upper front teeth, or when there is a large space between the upper and lower front teeth) will distort certain sounds such as S, V, F and Th, making crisp diction impossible. A good orthodontist can correct any irregularities. Your teeth should *never* be touching when you speak.

Protrude your tongue between your teeth, far enough so that you could take a good healthy bite off the tip of it. Now roll it back slowly until it touches the hard roof of your mouth behind your upper teeth (your hard palate). Continue to roll it back until the tip touches the soft, pulpy area behind your hard palate (your soft palate). Your tongue needs this much flexibility to produce precisely the sounds of T, D, N, L and Th.

Place two fingers between your teeth. Bite gently on your fingers, holding your jaw opened to this degree while mentally counting slowly to ten. Your jaw should not begin to ache or feel tense. If it does, it may indicate that you have become a victim of "lazy" speech and you are not using enough movement in your jaw when articulating. Practice saying out loud ah — ee — ah — ee — ah — ee. There should be a definite opening and closing motion in your jaw. Be sure you do not close your jaws completely on the ee sound. If you do not relax and move your lower jaw easily, you will find some articulation drills at the end of this chapter for you to practice.

Finally, and this test is very important, check to discover any nasal quality in your voice. Few impediments are so obvious and so damaging to a speaker. Simply place your index finger beside one nostril and press it closed. Breathe three or four times through the opened nostril, conscious of the amount of breath you are using. Now, reverse the procedure by blocking the opposite nostril and again, breathe in and out several times. Both should feel *exactly* the same. The same amount of air should pass through, unobstructed, on each side. If you think you can detect any obstruction on either side, check with an ear, nose and throat specialist to determine the cause, and the alternatives to removal. A blockage may interfere with the pronunciation of the nasal sounds M, N and NG. If you have discovered no physical blockage, but you feel you may have a little nasal twang in your voice, the exercises that follow in this chapter for eliminating a nasal sound are especially for you; although everyone should try them for consistent improvement.

Having determined that all is well, you are ready to proceed. The next step is to discover your own individual base tone and to understand why that is the most important foundation on which to create an impressive speaking voice.

## Why Establish a Basic Tone?

Have you ever found yourself commenting on a TV or radio personality and saying, "I cannot stand that woman." What you mean is not that you hold a dislike for the woman, whom you don't know, but that her voice grates on your ears and you find it taxing to listen to her.

Everyone felt some sympathy for the well-intentioned, long-suffering Edith Bunker on "All in the Family," but few could listen to her comfortably.

You realize that the women who broadcast the news are reading from a pre-written script, and are simply repeating someone else's words, but the newscaster's voice is still the standard bearer of her own personality and it gives a clear message about her own attitudes and disposition, and it overrides her material. You accept or reject her as a person, not on the content of the nightly news, nor on the blouse and jacket she is wearing, but on her voice. You like her because she sounds sincere and authoritative. She projects this image through the rich, pleasant tones in her speech.

A voice in the lower ranges immediately telegraphs a sense of believability. Try saying, "It is time to leave," in a high squeaky voice. Now repeat it in much deeper tones. Isn't there a surprising difference? No wonder the mother who talks in a rich, positive voice commands obedience, while the more high pitched, nervous woman is repeating her wishes to deaf ears.

Lower tones are more pleasant to listen to and they are much easier for most people to hear. This is especially true for most elderly people and anyone with a slight hearing disability. You will find the reasons for this explained in the chapter on "Talking With The Hard of Hearing."

You will also establish credibility more easily if you present your material in the lower ranges. They are simply far more convincing. Prove this to yourself. Say out loud in high quick tones,

"Women have achieved leadership in many fields. They have earned the right of recognition."

Repeat it in a deeper, more deliberate manner. No matter which way it is said, the statement is true, but wouldn't others be apt to believe the second delivery you made more readily? You will never hear a truly charismatic speaker using thin, high pitched tones.

## How to Determine the Right Pitch for You

Your most flattering and effective voice will emerge from your diaphragm, through a relaxed, open throat. It is much easier to understand how it is arrived at, than it is to produce it. As soon as you become tense, the muscles in your stomach react first, and soon the palms of your hands become moist, and your throat begins to tighten. Your voice sky-rockets! The more tense you become, the higher your voice climbs. If you become engulfed in enough emotion, you'll find that you cannot speak at all. This will never do. To reach the goal you are striving for, you must first relax your throat.

Simulate a yawn. Draw your breath in over and over in huge gulps, until you are able to yawn easily, and you will feel all your throat muscles tense then relax. Now, with your throat completely opened, hit down hard on your vocal cords with the deepest loudest HOO or WHOO you can muster. This is a noisy exercise. If you can't be heard in every room in your home, you are not doing it correctly. Get it down deep and loud. Try it again. Repeat it again, over and over, until it no longer sounds like your own voice, but a giant shouting at you from the cellar. Try it again —

Yawn — Yawn, relax your throat.

Now, deep breathe through the mouth and WHO — HOO — HOO — WHOO. Push it out — deep and forceful — project all the way to your neighbor's house. No "lady like" sound this — it's a whopping exclamation.

Once you feel you are truly down there, and take your time making that decision, then you are ready to find, with ease, your best speaking voice.

Start by reciting the letters of the alphabet, with "A" on the deepest tone you have reached in the previous exercise. Now, start with your voice climbing up a speaking note at a time.

                 E
              D
          C
       B
    A

If you are doing it correctly, between the C and D is the perfect basic tone for you. You will probably find it is a little deeper and richer than the tone you have been using, especially the tone you employ when you are ill at ease. But this is the tone you want to develop, and while it is vital that you never speak in a monotone, and your speaking voice have the same flexibility as your singing voice, it is paramount that you know the location of your individual "middle C."

Now that you have found it, employ it. Use it when you say "hello," "thank you," "yes, please," and "good bye." Be aware that when you wish to command obedience, you need only drop it a tone or two.

Junior, come home
                *now!*

It must be finished
                *today!*

You are employing a powerful force here. Entire nations are swayed by the convincing, authoritarian, powerful, enthusiastic and all encompassing voice of one person. You may not wish to change a nation, but you hold the same key, and once you understand how to use it, you can make a substantial contribution in the area of your choice. You can lead if you choose to lead, or you can be equally dynamic in the support you give to those whom you wish to promote.

## Eliminate Any Nasal Tendency

The "sister sin" of the high, squeaky voice is the nasal voice. It is equally annoying to the listener and completely lacking in character. You can self-test for it and eliminate it quite easily by following these few easy steps.

There are only three sounds in our language that pass through the nasal cavities, M, N and Ng. All other sounds project from your diaphragm and vocal chords, through your mouth. If you have ever suffered from a bad cold, or allergies, you may suspect that every sound needs unclogged nasal passages, but in reality only the M, N and Ng are suffering.

Read the following sentence out loud.

Many men met in Memphis on Monday.

Now, pinch your nose closed with your thumb and index finger. *Be sure,* now, that you keep the palm of your hand directed away from your mouth, and the remaining fingers up toward your eyes. If you cover your mouth with your hand, you will distort the sounds you are trying to hear clearly. Now repeat the sentence with your nostrils closed. It is completely distorted. You will not only hear the blocked nasal sounds, you will also feel their vibrations in your fingers.

Without pinching your nostrils, repeat this sentence.

Please put the cat outside.

Again, pinching your nostrils closed, and keeping your hand above your mouth, repeat that sentence.

Because there is no nasal sound included, the sentence should sound exactly the same when you say it with your nostrils closed. Try it several times. Listen closely to the word "please," it is the one word most apt to give you trouble.

If you hear, or feel, that some of your breath is passing

through your nose, continue to block your nostrils and practice the following words and sentences, taking a shallow breath before each word and blowing it directly through your mouth. Repeat this exercise several times daily, until you rid yourself completely of any tendency to misdirect your breath. It is one of the easiest of all difficulties to overcome, and rewards you with startling, dramatic results. It is well worth your concentration and effort.

Read from left to right:

| *Hear and feel the nasal tone* | *Completely free of any nasal sound* |
|---|---|
| Now | How |
| Never | Ever |
| May | Way |
| Might | Sight |
| Near | Hear |

Be equally careful when the sound comes at the end of a word.

| Spurn | Spirit |
|---|---|
| Loon | Loop |
| Loosen | Loose |
| Drum | Drug |
| Pin | Pill |

These sentences have no M, N or Ng, and should sound the same when you block your nostrils:

The actor said "Stop!"
The horse reared.
Good! You did it well!

## Articulation Drills

We have only 26 letters in our alphabet and only about 40 sounds in our language. Of these sounds, eight are voiceless or whispered sounds, so it becomes increasingly obvious that we must pronounce all of our sounds clearly, if we are to be easily understood. This means we must give some thought to how well we articulate. We must use our tongue and lips and jaw to form each word concisely. Articulation, in conjunction with expression, forms our verbal punctuation. Here are some of the sounds we are most likely to slur. Once you think about how they are formed, and you say them out loud, feeling them being projected, you will recognize any that you have been careless in articulating. You will soon notice an improvement, and you will become comfortable using your tongue and your lips and jaw to reinforce what you are saying.

P and B are explosive sounds. They are both made by pressing your lips together and exploding them with your breath. They are exactly the same, except that B is voiced, and P is a whispered sound. Combine them with the vowels and pronounce them slowly, feeling exactly how they are formed. Pa — Pe — Pi — Po — Pu : Ba — Be — Bi — Bo — Bu. Paper — Pumpkin — Puppy : Baby — Bluebird — Bubble.

F and V are also formed exactly alike. (Sounds produced in the same way, with one sound voiced and the other whispered are called cognates.) This pair is created by placing your upper teeth on your lower lip and forcing your breath through. F is voiceless, V is voiced. Again, say them out loud with the vowels, and pronounce them very slowly. Fa, Fe, Fi, Fo, Fu/Va, Ve, Vi, Vo, Vu. Fifty, Fulfill, Fife/Vivid, Vacation, Verve.

T, D, N and L are great sounds. They sharpen our language for us. For each of these sounds, your tongue must touch the roof of your mouth. No lazy sounds these! Feel your tongue clicking on the roof of your mouth as you combine this set of consonants with vowels. Ta, Te, Ti, To, Tu/Da, De, Di, Do, Du/Na, Ne, Ni, No. Nu/La, Le, Li, Lo, Lu.

| Tutor  | Diddle | Nana | Loll |
| Title  | Deed   | Nine | List |
| Tattle | Dud    | None | Lily |

We could not possibly bypass the most obviously mispronounced sound of all. If the "Th" is not articulated correctly it jumps out as a glaring error. There are two "th's". They too are cognates; one whispered, one voiced. The important thing to remember on this sound is that the tongue *must* be placed between the teeth to produce it correctly. This is the most difficult sound for many to whom English is a new language. Be sure you can bite gently down on your tongue when you recite the following drill.

Whispered: Tha, The, Thi, Tho, Thu
Think, Thank, Thought
Voiced: Tha, The, Thi, Tho, Thu
This, That, These

One final word; the last sound in all words is equal in importance to the initial sound. Be sure you give it its due.

## Multi-Syllable Words

Another helpful exercise in improving your articulation is simply to take any series of multi-syllable words and pronounce them slowly, exaggerating each syllable. Try these, then make up your own additional list. (You might start with additional.)

Administration: Ad — min — is — tra — tion
Inadvertently: In — ad — vert — ent — ly
Individualistic: In — di — vid — u — al — is — tic
Voluminous: Vo — lu — mi — nous
Interchangeable: In — ter — change — able

The next time someone presents you with a tongue twister, simply say it precisely, forming every one of the repeated sounds individually; that will prevent them from slurring together and twisting you up, and your accurate articulation will astound them!

More important — the dividends you will gain from reviewing the exercises in this chapter, and working consistently each day to improve your voice and your delivery, will be reflected in your business image, in your social and personal life, and in your increased assurance and self-esteem. It is the best investment of time and effort you can possibly make to advance positively toward your own personal goal. Begin today.

# Chapter Three

## Parties are Supposed to be Fun; But are They?

A party, according to Mr. Webster's dictionary, is, "a company of persons for social enjoyment, entertainment and a joyful gathering." The purpose, it seems is to relax and enjoy, but for many women it often becomes a somewhat taxing period of time. They say they are often apprehensive before they arrive, uneasy when they are there, and tense and uncertain of the impression they made when they left. Is it because they feel they are unattractive in their appearance? Not usually. There is no excuse for any woman to be less than striking today, and most do feel satisfied with their individual style. If not, help is available on all sides; excellent hairstylists, expert make-up advisors, and competent fashion co-ordinators are all standing by to give aid and advice where it is needed. Any woman, absolutely any woman, can enter a room today and attract admiring attention by her appearance. There is no secret to looking your best. The woman who holds and builds on that initial impression is the one who speaks well, is at ease in her conversation and thereby allows those around her to feel comfortable. How does she manage to do that? Probably by a little extra preparation. If you feel that others are having more fun at parties than you are, let's explore a well thought out approach that will have you looking forward with confidence to meeting new people.

When you receive an invitation, either by mail or phone, you probably take several automatic steps. You check your calendar, accept with pleasure, phone your hairdresser, give some thought to what you will wear, and then, depending on your present station in life, call a babysitter or arrange for transportation. If that is the extent of your preparation, you are just short of assuring yourself of a pleasant evening. Take one more step and see the difference a little thought given to your voice and your speech will make.

Begin, if possible, by knowing who some of the other guests will be. If you know even two or three, you can make mental notes of topics you would enjoy discussing with them, and you will be assured of starting the evening in a comfortable atmosphere. If your hostess phones you, she will probably identify some of the others who will be included, and you can jot down notes and review them again that evening before you leave home. It is a great aid in starting conversations. When Jan Jackson is introduced to you, you are ready to say sincerely, "I've been looking forward to meeting you, Jan. Susan told me you just returned from Moscow and I'm interested in your impression of Russian women." You are then on your way to a most interesting conversation.

If you have no way of knowing ahead anything about any of the guests, a thoughtful hostess will always add a bit more than just names to an introduction and you can pick up your cue from her. She may say, "I'd like to have to meet Betty Long, another avid gardener," and again you have a great starting point.

What happens if you enter a room of strangers and there is no one to introduce you? To whom should you speak? You may join any group and introduce yourself. The fact that you have all been invited is, in itself, an umbrella introduction and a sponsoring of each person there by the host and hostess.

## Starting a Conversation

There are three basic ways to start a conversation. After introducing yourself you may tell a little bit about yourself and your relationship to the hostess. "Susan and I are working together this year on the Symphony Ball. She is working on the invitations, and I am responsible for the decorations." Someone will then ask you a question or tell you a bit about herself.

Or, you may ask a general question, but if you choose that approach, be sure it cannot be answered by a simple yes or no, or you may not start a conversation. It is better to begin with, "What did you think of the successful fireworks display last night? Should we make it an annual event?" than to ask, "Aren't the hors d'oeuvres delicious?"

A sincere compliment is always a gracious way to begin. "I have been admiring your cameo. They have always been a favorite of mine and that shade of blue is lovely." It must be a compliment, not empty flattery. If it is not direct and sincere it is best not to offer it. Bishop Fulton J. Sheen said it best. "A compliment is baloney so thinly sliced it is delicious, flattery is baloney cut so thick it is indigestible."

Conversations are much easier to start if you are a multi-topic person. Many things should be of interest to you, and you should always remain well-read and abreast of current events. Have several topics ready so that when a lull threatens to descend, you can prevent it by asking, "What are your views on the proposed new Civic Center? Do you think it will raise the revenue the mayor hopes for?" Matters that interest and concern you, interest and concern others, also, and most people are willing to share their opinions on public issues. Reading the daily newspaper and keeping up on the newest books will not only make you well-read, but also with a little forethought, well-spoken. Arrive at your next social function armed with topics and notice how much easier the dialogue flows.

As important as what you say is the quality and clarity of your voice. Never strident or whining, but projected from your relaxed, opened throat in your lower ranges, it will be pleasing, inviting, and it will encourage others to join with you. The rule of thumb says you should be able to project your voice, without strain, about 15 feet. You will certainly not need this volume in conversation, but in a crowded room with distracting noises, you will want to speak up enough to be heard easily. Be sure you are wearing a smile, because it is most becoming to your voice. Develop the habit of looking directly at the person with whom you are speaking. With the "do's" come the "don'ts" and it is well to keep a few in mind.

Don't touch people when speaking with them.
Don't become redundant in your speech.
Don't attempt to make a derogatory remark under the guise of humor.
Don't attempt to shock.

Conversations at parties should be kept light and positive. Subjects with depth and of interest can promote stimulating exchanges, but lengthy, emotional debates won't contribute to a good time. Death, politics, religion, illness, children and dogs usually head the list of subjects to be avoided, but there are exceptions to all rules. By watching the person with whom you are speaking, you will know at once when the conversation is pleasing. There is a story often told about Winston Churchill that left little doubt as to a subject in which he had no interest. It is said that a gentleman remarked to him one day, "Mr. Churchill, do you realize we have known each other for several months now and I have never told you about my grandchildren?" "I certainly do" replied the statesman, "and I can't tell you how grateful I am!"

But general rules are helpful and if you want to rate your own conversational ability, try scoring yourself on the following composite test.

When speaking with new acquaintances, do I:

- Look at the person with whom I am speaking?
- Avoid monopolizing the conversation?
- Pay strict attention and concentrate?
- Have a variety of topics that interest me?
- Tell a humorous story well, or omit it?
- Refrain from topping every story I hear?
- Try not to force my opinion?
- Discipline myself not to anger easily?
- Avoid overfamiliarity and personal questions?
- Make an effort to help in conversational lulls?
- Ask thoughtful questions?
- Elect not to discuss shortcomings in others?
- Abstain from reciting my pet peeves and problems?
- Try never to interrupt?
- Attempt to avoid a direct contradiction?
- Improve my speaking voice?
- Make an honest effort to understand the things that interest others?
- Employ the proper volume for the occasion?
- Smile easily?
- Sincerely care and show it?

If you had fewer than 15 yes answers, you need to apply a serious effort toward improving your conversational habits.

No matter how seriously you try, not all conversations can be made into engaging discussions. Eventually, even good visits come to an end. Sometimes, people are called away and you are suddenly alone. It's time to move on.

If the discussion has come to a termination point, tell the guests how much you have enjoyed talking with them, say you hope to see them again later, and go to greet other friends. Be sure your tone of voice and your smile reaffirms that you have enjoyed meeting them.

If you suddenly find yourself alone, do something. If the party is not catered, pass the cheese tray, or help the hostess if she is away from the door by greeting late arrivals and making them feel welcome. Join another group or sample something new on the buffet table. Become visible again, try being as useful as you are ornamental, but don't just stand alone waiting to be entertained. Use your well-modulated voice to seek out new acquaintances. Not everyone you meet will become a life-long friend, but you can be certain that your list of friends will grow.

## Meeting a Celebrity

People who would normally engage others in an easy, graceful conversation sometimes stand in awe of a celebrity. Completely tongue-tied, they fail to contribute to even a token conversation. It is really not such a difficult situation.

If you know in advance that a well-known person will be the guest speaker for the evening, or among the guests at a party, do a little homework. If you will be meeting a well-known author, try to read her latest book (and be sure it is *her* book and that you have the correct title.) Start as you would with any other new acquaintance, by expressing an interest in her work and a sincere compliment. Yes, probably a dozen others have already told her they enjoyed the book, but the recognition is still appreciated. You might ask a guest speaker about her schedule or the difference she has found in audiences in various parts of the country. She, too, wants to be included.

## Excessive Drinkers

No one improves with liquor. Neither her speech, nor her voice nor her thinking process can do anything but deteriorate. Even that rare person, who seems at first to become the life of the party, after a few additional drinks is soon more laughed at than with — which is in itself sad. What should you do when you are cornered and uncomfortable? Make an excuse and move on. You may find it is time to help your hostess, call home to check with the sitter, or any other excuse that calls for immediate action. If your pleasant voice and charm put you into this predicament, allow your firm authoritative tones to extract you from it.

## The Casanova

What do you say, and in what tone of voice, when the self-appointed Casanova of the evening turns out to be your neighbor's husband or the vice-president of your firm? Dozens of snappy remarks have been published and, although they are great reading, they seldom seem appropriate when the situation arises. You'd rather not make an enemy, but enough is enough. A smile over a good, firm deep tone that says, "Absolutely, that is the end" and an immediate lapse of memory on the whole foolish matter, still seems to be best and most expedient. Then move on.

If it is your party, be sure you keep it manageable. Try not to engage in long conversations in order to assure that all your guests receive your attention and are comfortable. Give a verbal helping hand to those who find conversation difficult and start those whom you introduce off with a conversation launcher, by mentioning common interests or giving a little background on each one.

With a little advance thought, planning and attention to the things you will be saying, and the voice you will be using to express them, your inner confidence will grow and you will enjoy the others as they will enjoy you. Then, when you walk into the room, looking your best, everyone will say, "My, isn't she attractive," but when you leave you'll receive the far more important compliment of, "My, isn't she an interesting and gracious person!" That is the compliment you want — that's the compliment you must work for — and that is the compliment you are capable of receiving.

# Chapter Four

## Personal Introductions

The staid formalities of life are fast disappearing and the rigid rules of strict society are gradually dissolving into a more comfortable, relaxed atmosphere as a younger generation emerges. Personal introductions, like so much of our etiquette today, sensibly revolve around simply making the other person feel comfortable. It requires only minimum effort to introduce two people and start them on a mutually interesting and productive conversation. Any small clue to a common interest or aid in establishing the clear identity of each person will do. For example: "Mother, I would like to have you meet Mary Alice Stuart," doesn't give enough information to either party. Instead, "Mother, I would like you to meet Mary Alice Stuart. We work together preparing the publicity releases for the company, and the article you admired in Sunday's paper was primarily her suggestion."

There will be times when you will find yourself in more formal situations. You will be more relaxed and self-confident if you know the exact rules of etiquette. They may seem a bit stilted and seldom employed, but being familiar with them and able to comfortably implement them when necessary, will enhance your self-confidence noticeably. The standard set for formal introductions is relatively simple. Just remember that what you are doing is asking the permission of one person, the person of greater age or accomplishment, to present another person whom you are sponsoring. All will be well if you always start with the name of the person of greater age or position. Use the full name of both parties and titles should always be included in introductions, allowing the people who earned them the prerogative of dismissing them if they so choose.

Start with the woman's name first when presenting a gentleman (unless the woman is under eighteen). The only time a woman is ever presented to a man is when the man is the President of the United States, a head of state, royal personage or church dignitary. You name the clergy always before the laymen, the older person preceeds the younger, and the honored guest before the members of the party. Try it with the combinations given below. Underline the person's name you should say first; then check your answers on the next page.

1. your daughter your female friend
2. The Bishop your husband
3. your female friend your husband
4. young man your daughter
5. elderly aunt your female friend
6. mayor (male) your son
7. doctor (male) your female friend
8. male friend your mother
9. female friend your father
10. honored male guest your brother
11. your boss (female) your father
12. your boss (male) your mother
13. doctor (female) elderly aunt

If you managed to answer ten out of thirteen correctly, then you are doing very well, indeed. More importantly, if those whom you entertain feel comfortable, sincerely welcome and enjoy your hospitality, you are pretty close to social perfection.

Answers to quiz: 1. female friend 2. Bishop 3. female friend 4. daughter 5. elderly aunt 6. mayor 7. female friend 8. your mother 9. female friend 10. honored male guest 11. your boss 12. your mother 13. elderly aunt

# Chapter Five

## Job Interview

Never is it more personally important to you to have confidence in your speaking voice and to do your homework than before a job interview. You may be able to obtain "work" just by showing up and looking neat and clean, but when you take your first step into the "career" world you will need to offer more to your prospective employer. As soon as you set your sights on the company and the position you want, it is time to begin to consider the positive impression your voice will create and to do a thorough job of preparation to reinforce it.

Of course, you should give thought to what you will wear, but that is so obvious that there is little need to go into it beyond the point of reminding you to check that your dress is consistent with the position for which you are applying. Never overdress. You should be absolutely positive before you arrive at the office that your appearance will not detract from your opportunity, but beyond that it is not going to be the deciding factor. Overshadowing all else on that day will be your voice and your speech because they showcase your attitudes and your potential for leadership.

To paraphrase Shakespeare — Neither a whisperer nor a shouter be — for a whisperer loses both assurance and confidence, and a shouter dulls the edge of competency. Again and again the value of a well modulated, clear voice in your natural lower range (which you found in the chapter "A Speech Class For One") cannot be overemphasized. It is your greatest asset. It will establish immediately the tone of the entire interview, and ultimately determine the interviewer's most important consideration — will you fit into their organization? Review, also, some supplementary steps which you can take to assure a successful interview.

### Homework

The very first guarantee of success is being completely sure you can handle the job you are seeking. If you know you would like the position, but have any question about your qualifications, reinforce your resumé before applying. Be sure that not only are your goals correctly set, but also that the timing is right for you.

Check, also, that this company is the one to which you should be applying and the one best suited to your talents. Next to your marriage and your family, your job will consume the largest part of every day, and those are a great many hours to commit to the wrong job. Research every aspect of the firm. If it is a small concern, about which no book has been written, head for the periodicals in the public library and you may find an article — or at least some material in professional journals — on a similar institution. Know all you can about the people for whom you will be working — ask others already employed there about the policies of the company and what they look for and expect from their employees. How would your interests and expertise fit into its framework?

Think a bit about salary. How much can you reasonably expect? How much are they paying others in comparable positions? You should have a general figure in mind even before you fill out the application, as that question is often asked on the initial form.

Anticipate the questions which will most likely be asked of you and have your answers ready. The interviewer may insert one or two inquiries which are totally unexpected such as, "What makes you angry?", but you will be able, with a little thought, to predict most questions beforehand. You will be expected to talk about former employment — starting with your last job first. Know what you want to say about your reasons for leaving and resolve that you will refrain from any derogatory remarks about either the company policies or its personnel.

You may reasonably expect any prospective employer to ask these two questions; why do you want to join our firm? and, what unique qualities or contributions do you feel you can offer to it? (You remember how it hurt Ted Kennedy when he was asked on TV why he wanted to be President, and he couldn't at once come up with an answer. Don't let this happen to you.)

If you have any material which will be helpful in showing what you have done, or can do, be sure to have it with you. Include all salient facts that make you valuable.

Be sure to allow yourself plenty of time so that you will arrive a minute or two early — despite the traffic tie-up, the already-filled parking garage, and the two elevators which were not working. If you are already frustrated, tense and nervous when you arrive, it will show in your voice and the resulting high, tight sound will lower your compatability rating.

## When You Arrive

Walk toward your interviewer with a quick, firm step and look directly at her as you shake hands. Meet her with your most pleasant voice and positive manner. (This is just one of the countless times when you will find that your well-modulated voice will pay big dividends.)

Restrict any preliminary social conversation to a short

period of time. Compliments on her clothes, jewelry, or the office decor are out of order here.

Your interviewer will probably want you to sit and talk with her, but it is customary to remain standing until she asks you to be seated. If you then have your choice between a soft chair and a straight one, be sure to sit in the straight chair, as it will be more graceful to get in and out of, and it will improve your posture and in turn, your voice.

Don't fidget. Relax your hands in your lap and keep them quiet. Appear calm and composed. In speech classes the students are asked if the speaker "appeared" calm and in control. She will usually say she was shaking inside, but she is rated only on how she appears. You will be, too.

Answer all questions with more than a monosyllable if possible — they do want to know about you. This is not the time for excessive modesty. If she says "I see you worked on your college newspaper," it is perfectly correct to answer, "Yes, one year as an editorial writer and two years as editor. They were good years and we were able to double our subscriptions during that time." But, while all businesses are looking for people who will help the company to progress, they may not be searching in this interview for someone to take over and run it singlehandedly. Again, your tone of voice in answering all questions should stay in your natural lower ranges and should say, "I have ability and I am willing to learn. I am a competent and pleasing person. I will become a strong *part of your team.*" If your voice is saying, "I am so competitive that I can be bold and arrogant and strident. Just let me show you how I can shake up your status quo," your tones may easily defeat you. Enthusiasm is shown with color and tempo, not with strong belligerence. Many a position has been awarded to someone slightly less qualified, but who sold herself to the interviewer as being able to work harmoniously with the established personnel.

This is not the time for you to ask a string of questions about vacation time, coffee breaks, benefits, etc. However, you should feel free to inquire about activities and services which the company offers, and its policy on reimbursing employees for additional education credits. Of course, if this job involves a move for you to a new city, there will be another set of questions you will want to include.

With your voice and your manner you must assure the interviewer not only that you want to work but also that you are willing to learn and adopt the company's methods, and that you are easy to get along with and capable of handling responsibility. Remember, the interviewer already knows your qualifications — she is looking at your personality and adaptability.

Never, under any circumstances, recite your hard luck stories. No one should feel intimidated, harrassed or pressured into accepting your application.

If the interview takes place in an open office, be sure you only pay attention to the person with whom you are speaking. Resist any temptation to look around to see what others are doing.

There are a wide variety of opinions among women today on their feelings about answering questions which are now illegal to ask. They range from — "the rights of the employer have been violated, — if they are investing a great deal of money in training you, they should be able to ask questions they feel will affect your efficiency on the job" to — "I simply say I prefer not to answer questions bordering on my personal life. I'll take care of all personal concerns outside of office hours." In between are the vast group of practical souls who have decided it depends a great deal on how much they want the job, and as long as no one is asking them to apologize for anything, simply to state a true fact, they have nothing to hide, and so feel no resentment. How you choose to deal with these questions is a personal matter, but you should know your rights and alternatives and make your decision from a knowledgeable base.

When the interviewer indicates the interview is over, thank her for her time, and leave promptly. If she doesn't tell you when you will be notified, it is perfectly acceptable to ask when you may expect to hear a decision. If considerable extra time has been spent with you, or special thoughtfulness shown, then a thank you note is in order and always appreciated.

## If You Conduct the Interview

Once again, your voice plays a major role. You may miss the best applicant on the list if your tone is so abrasive that you intimidate her, or so weak and listless that she decides your company is not dynamic enough. You are representing an entire company. How your image comes across the desk is vital. All the suggestions for checking and improving your voice are of paramount importance in your position.

If you are working in a large company, you are already trained in its format. If you are with a small concern, or starting out in your own business, this may be a totally new duty for you. Perhaps it can be made a bit easier with these general suggestions.

Try to put the applicant at ease immediately. You will get a much more productive response. Just a few general words of greeting are all that is necessary.

Give her a complete job description. If you decide to employ her, her first week should not be full of surprises.

Set aside time to give her your full attention. Do not interrupt the interview unless it is unavoidable.

Expect her to have questions about the work, and be prepared to answer them fully.

Take the time to read her application before she arrives and know as much about her in advance as you can.

Let her know your decision as soon as possible. If you are certain she is not qualified for the job by the time the interview is over, tell her, and thank her for her interest.

When you feel you have all the information you need to make a decision, thank her sincerely and bring the interview to an end.

# Chapter Six

## Tips for the Career Woman

### Looking Toward Advancement

If you have already decided on a career and entered your chosen field, or a related one with plans to work from there to your goal, then you are now looking toward promotions. As a businesswoman with your eyes on career advancement, you should be particularly aware of your speaking voice. A pleasant voice, easy to listen to, with tones in your natural lower ranges, to project a knowledgeable assurance, and the absence of any rasping nasal irritations is the best possible investment for you to pursue. (See "A Speech Class For One.")

You should not only accept, but seek out every opportunity to stand before a group and establish your own comfortable style of address. You should start doing this now — while you still have a chance to practice at a relatively minor level, and mistakes are not catastrophic. If you do not take hold of the reins and plunge forward now, no matter how you may dread trying, someday this one shortcoming will rise up as a hurdle of immense proportions. This cannot be urged too strongly. If you were to make only one effort, in one area, to help yourself to success, there is absolutely nothing that would be so important as speaking up and speaking well. It is equally applicable to all fields. Those dealing with office statistics, computers or research projects stand to profit as fully as those who are salespeople, teachers, consultants or in advertising and personnel. When you attend conventions, who is at the head table? Those who not only know their field, but also can speak out, explain it and offer their ideas for the future of their industry. Why not be a chief? No one has ever proven that the Indians have more fun!

Climb the Ladder with a Succession<br>of Easy Basic Steps.

Stay alert — watch and listen. What are they telling you, those at the top? What direction are they moving in? What can you contribute to that momentum? If you are only making your "Wouldn't you think they would . . ." suggestions to those on your own level, they are worthless. If it is only as you are walking out the door of a meeting that you ask the person you came with, "I wonder why they didn't . . ." it's a zero question. Don't even bother to ask it then. It counts for absolutely nothing. It might have been a big plus for your career if your question or suggestion had been introduced appropriately a few minutes before. Speak up.

Be enthused! You may not have heard an old song of the 40's that gave some first class advice for the 80's, but it went like this. "Accentuate the positive — Eliminate the negative — Latch onto the affirmative — Don't mess with Mr. In between." Again, there is not a single vocation where speaking out and speaking well is not a basic ingredient for success. Students in colleges and universities throughout the country who are now asked to rate the faculty yearly, consistently list lack of enthusiasm and animation as their number one complaint. A teacher, so bored with her subject that she presents it in a monotone, is a disgrace to her profession. The businesswoman who allows her job and her voice to become dull and routine should offer her resignation at once. She has absolutely nothing more to offer her company. If you have the opportunity to enroll in a Public Speaking course, don't hesitate. Be sure your instructor gives you a critique of your voice as well as your delivery. If you studied Public Speaking in college, and that was more than two years ago, try it again. Each instructor has slightly different approaches and something uniquely her own to offer. Stay current.

## Training Others and Giving Instructions
### A Good Starting Point

Everyone is asked to give instructions in one form or another. You may be training a new employee, helping a temporary replacement, showing a new procedure or explaining a new piece of equipment. Strive to develop the elementary ability of giving clear and specific explanations and reports in a well-modulated voice. It will be a vital necessity at every level of management. Whether you are teaching one person, or handling an entire training program, here are some rules to follow that will make you a more competent leader.

Organize and outline ahead all the points you wish to cover. Lay out and diagram all work formulas in a manner that compels co-operation. Have handouts ready with details repeated.

Tell it first to your tape recorder and listen to your inflections. Are you going to be understood easily?

Be sure you are thoroughly familiar with all aspects of the procedures and can explain all directions in detail. Give all directions in strict chronological order — never back track.

Expect unrelated questions as well as those directly concerning your subject and answer all with patience and courtesy. Always encourage questions.

Don't assume anyone knows everything. Be watchful that your tone is not condescending, but explain each step from the beginning.

Never elect only to talk if you can demonstrate, and never demonstrate unless you are 100% familiar with the equipment and the way it works. Know how to fix it if it doesn't work. It can be embarrassing if you have to call someone to come and operate the gadget you are explaining.

Repeat and rephrase, working always from the familiar to the new.

Speak a fraction more slowly, but never talk down to your listeners.

Be sure to clarify all "office lingo" and give a definition for all technical terms.

Keep eye contact. Make it a point to look at each individual and it will pin-point those in trouble for you.

It is not ever necessary to engage in any rhetoric, praising or criticizing the company's procedures. Explain them in a positive manner without personal comment. In answering any question, always express the company policy. If you do not give the business that employs you your complete support, you are cheating it.

Volunteer to give instructions whenever you have the opportunity. If you are to hold a leadership position of authority, you must be able to communicate directions. Be willing and look for ways to assume responsibility outside of your immediate areas of assignment, and opportunities for you to become of greater value. Speak before small groups and at meetings whenever possible. Make each presentation productive by expanding the value of the material with your commanding presentation. Even a man of the magnificent mettle of Abraham Lincoln was not fully appreciated in his lifetime, partly because the delivery of his speeches fell so far short of the worth of their content. Those who stood on the fields at Gettysburg had no idea of the astute message they were hearing until it was later published. Most people do not have a second chance to reach their listeners — they must accomplish their aim the first time.

All companies are interested in building goodwill. Perhaps you can help by speaking to church, school and community groups about the work that is currently being done in your organization, and their plans for the future. You may, also, be able to contribute additional exposure for your company by working in their name with the Chamber of Commerce or the United Fund. Don't be afraid to be visible, and don't postpone improving your speaking image.

Again and again it is necessary to deal with the human fear of criticism. Being unwilling to be thought of by co-workers as a company person — afraid to look like an apple polisher by taking on extra work and feeling uncomfortable about progressing faster than other employees; that is a decision you must make. If you wish to remain static and one of the crowd, you do not need to expand a weak voice and halting speech patterns. To become a leader you must sound like one and create. Is there a price to pay? Perhaps, depending upon your personal viewpoint. Does it mean you have to trample over others, spew out aggressiveness and be concerned only with yourself? Must you scheme and contrive? No. It means making a decision within yourself — striving honestly to improve, weighing and incorporating constructive criticism and rising above pettiness. The more you allow yourself to worry about what others think, the less you will do. The less you strive to do, and do well, the more their opinions of you will falter.

Abraham Lincoln once said: "If I tried to read, much less answer all the criticisms made of me, and all the attacks leveled against me, this office would be closed for all other business. I do the best I know how, the very best I can, and I mean to keep on doing this to the end."

If you choose to reach for higher goals, begin. If you make a conscious decision not to, fine, but then determine that you will give a word of encouragement and honest support to those who are trying to improve. They deserve all the help you can give them, for they are working hard to produce to their potential. They'll appreciate your backing sincerely, and you will still come out a winner, because some day you will have friends in high places.

## The Business Meeting

At a college seminar for businesswomen, the poorest and most unprofessional advice was given by a woman listed as an executive with an insurance company. She rose to give her address and started by saying, "The first thing you'd better learn when attending a meeting is how to sleep with your eyes opened." Most of the audience smiled and waited for the punch line. There was none. She went on telling about how she compiled her grocery list, etc. during office meetings, and how, when she was caught by someone asking her a question, she'd simply ask to have the question repeated. She admitted that sometimes her answers didn't have much continuity with what was going on, but she explained "Usually, I'm able to fumble through." Most of the women turned her off at that point and started on their own grocery lists. Half an hour later she announced a ten minute break, after which she would continue, a fully two-thirds of the audience left, and looked for all the world like women headed for the grocery store. It is doubtful if she is still with the same company — or any company.

According to a study done recently at Ohio State University, executives spend 70% of their working time in some form of communications. More than 50% of this time is used listening to others. They are very good at it. They may doodle with a pen, but they are not making out grocery lists. They listen attentively. (This would be a good time to review the chapter "Let's Look At The Way You Listen".)

You may be at a point in your career where you are just beginning to be invited to sit in on certain meetings, or you may wish to sharpen your input and make some additional efforts to gain the most benefit from the conferences you now attend. Give some consideration to the following rules of thumb and you will find you will increase the value of the time spent and you will have taken some definite steps toward your own personal advancement.

If you are the person calling for the meeting, be sure you accurately define its purpose when you announce it. Avoid, "I want everyone to meet in Jane's office at 9:00 tomorrow morning. I've got some things I want to go over with you." Better: "All personnel concerned with the Water Purification Project are to meet at 9:00 A.M. tomorrow, Thursday, in Jane Simons' office to review the reports from the Environmental Control Department. We will decide upon the time frame for completion of current projects. Copies of the reports will be delivered to your desks this afternoon."

A word about handouts. Whenever it is possible, you should distribute them in advance of the meeting to avoid those attending trying to read them while you're talking. Be sure to have extras at the meeting for those who meant to bring them, but left them in their office.

If it is your meeting — lead it. Hold it on course — call a halt to talk on unrelated matters — don't allow one person to give a rhetorical monologue — and when you have come to the end of your outline of topics, thank those who came and then dismiss them.

If you are attending someone else's meeting, assume your share of responsibility and be prepared to contribute some worthwhile input. Try to remember that it has been called for the purpose of co-operation, not confrontation, and even though you are not in favor of "the Water Purification Project," it is not appropriate to march into the room like Grant taking Richmond.

If you want to create the image of a positive-thinking person, avoid presenting your ideas in a negative fashion. Which of the following opening remarks is more apt to gain group approval?

| | | |
|---|---|---|
| We probably shouldn't vote to spend this much money at this time, but . . . | -or- | The relative cost of this project is minor in comparison to . . . |
| This pump may look weak and flimsy and not structurally sound to you, but | -or- | The sturdiness of this small pump is amazing . . . |
| I'll grant it is difficult and you'll probably feel quite discouraged at first . . . | -or- | The amount of optimism you'll acquire in a short period of time . . . |
| Everyone knows there are some weaknesses to this approach, but . . . | -or- | The strengths of this plan are obvious . . . |
| We're not geared up to full-strength now and I'm not sure how many of these we can produce . . . | -or- | The exact number we can roll off the production line will be available soon . . . |

## Selling

This same approach applies to selling. So many women today are in the field offering goods that range from insurance policies to homes, it is only the most astute who will ultimately "super succeed." Never tell the prospective buyer, "The trouble with this house is," unless you're holding it for someone else. That is *not* saying, don't be honest — or shade your honesty. Never. It simply means be positive, and if there is "trouble" with anything or you feel what you have to offer may not be right for your customer in the long run, don't present it. You must first be convinced yourself — 100% sincerely convinced. You can develop self-confidence in your profession only after you have established self-respect.

Never employ "gimmicks" if you are seeking a sterling reputation. The more direct, straight-forward, well-documented your presentation, the more impressed a discerning client will be. Unless you're hawking at a side show, you will want to build on repeat business and a hallmark of integrity.

It is usually better to lose a sale than force or embarrass someone into making a purchase with which she is not completely satisfied. One negative advertisement can undo a great deal of hard work.

## When Should You Speak Up?

In the field or in the factory, the office or the lab, be ready to lead, to organize and to speak out in conferences and meetings, from the floor and from the podium. So often women feel intimidated, especially at meetings predominantly attended by male executives, and they want to speak up, but they're not sure when they should, and by the time they decide the matter, it's too late. They admit to repeated times of saying to themselves — "I wish I had spoken up." When these are the cir-

cumstances, then it's time to Speak Up:
- When you know you can clarify a point.
- When you can supplement pertinent information or furnish convincing statistics.
- When you can correct an error.
- When you wish to ask a question.
- When you can substantiate — or rebuke — a new procedure, a sales technique or a cost control.
- When you can give credit that's due.
- When you have a good idea, an original suggestion or a worthwhile appendage to contribute.
- When someone has taken your suggestion and tries to present it as her own.

If you just can't seem to start, try this method.

The very next time that you hear something said that is not crystal clear, ask the person presenting for a clarification. Stand to do this, if it is not inconsistent with the set-up of the meeting. It will accomplish several things for you. First, and most important, you have spoken up and successfully by-passed that "first time." You have shown that even though you are not a garrulous member, you are alert, interested and thinking. You have taken an active part and you have complimented the speaker with your attention. Now, remember, while congratulating yourself on this initial step, that this is a kindergarten graduation, and you are now requiring yourself to move right along rapidly.

Should someone correct or take issue with you during a meeting, never allow yourself to appear flustered or upset. Don't cease to contribute.

Assuming the correction or criticism is in order and presented politely, it should not deter you. Acknowledge it — stand corrected — admit a mistake — apologize graciously if it is in order — and move along. Do not review it again during the meeting — in the office later — at dinner that evening — or ever. It's settled — forget it. Sometimes a poor memory can be as helpful as a good one. The important thing is to maintain your dignity and your composure. Speak up again just as soon as it's appropriate.

We live in a highly competitive world. You must set goals for yourself and make plans for reaching them. To do so it is not necessary to be overly aggressive or abrasive. The woman with confirmed confidence, with well-thought out, positive statements, with the ability to speak with assurance, graciousness and clarity, will fulfil her ambitions and prove to be effective and respected. You can be that woman if you choose to be.

## The Business Talk

> Look to your speech, lest it mar your fortune.
> — Shakespeare

It is no longer just a polite request for women to speak about policies and directives, but a demand. Active women are called upon today from all fields to share their expertise as business associates, hospital directors, professional co-ordinators, board members, church group organizers, volunteers and political leaders. But you cannot share what you cannot express, and you certainly cannot convince if you cannot present. Nothing much can be accomplished if you do not squarely face the realization that being able to stand before a group of your peers, and addressing them effectively is an absolute necessity. This is the time to make up your mind that you will take your place among the "can do's!"

The fundamental rules for all forms of public speaking are the same, so your first step is to read the chapter title, "Of Course You Can Be A Guest Speaker," and underline all the points on which you feel the need to work, especially any corrections you feel necessary in your voice. The most carefully prepared presentation cannot get off the ground if your voice irritates, bores or fails to impress your audience. The class in Public Speaking in the Continuing Education Department of your local college should have your name on its roster. When you select a topic to speak on in class, instead of putting the effort into preparing five minutes on, "The Trip I Took Last Summer," offer instead, some topic which you might be called to speak on in your professional field. Imagine that your boss is to be the guest speaker, and introduce her to the class — your company is developing a new product, explain it — or if you have volunteered to train the new operators, this is the time to practice, pep talk and all. You think the class would be bored? You didn't sign up to entertain them; you're there to make some real progress in a difficult field, so begin. You may, ultimately, be surprised at the interest others will have in something that seems routine to you. Many students have been delightfully surprised at the peppy question periods that followed a speech they admitted they thought would be dull.

You have a tremendous advantage in a talk given either to people in your company or those in a related field. You know they are already interested in what you have to say. Now, that's a comfortable feeling, isn't it? (Don't sit there and answer, 'not really' — yes it is — be positive, admit it, take all the plusses you can get.) Also, this is the one time you do not have to assume that your audience has no previous background on your subject, so you don't have to review from block one — unless you are teaching. Another plus. You must still, of course, hold and develop their interest.

You will still need a good opening statement, but it's a little easier to compose. Be sure it is positive, and certainly never insulting to your listeners. Probably the all time poorest opening for any meeting is this, "Well, this is really off the top of my head. I haven't had much time to prepare anything for today, so I'll just fly and we'll see what happens." In one grand breath the speaker managed to tell everyone that she can't organized her time, she didn't think they were very important, she had better things to do than to show consideration for them, they are wasting their time by being there, and unless the good Lord declares it's "miracle time," absolutely nothing is apt to be accomplished. What a way to begin!

The advice on a strong closing statement given in the chapter, "How To Be A Great Speaker," is equally applicable. Never end your talk with, "Well, I guess that about covers it. I can't think of anything else to add. I hope I've explained it completely." Who would dare to ask a question after that? Your audience should be left anxious to ask questions, to support your position, or to act.

## An "Eloquent" Business Talk

When you are preparing the main body of your talk, remember, a good business address always follows an outline and topics are presented in chronological order. Be sure there is a clear understanding of the company policies on all matters you introduce. Tell them what they need to know, don't show-off how much you know. Bring it home. Make it clear how an increase in sales, or the incorporation of a new method, will affect your listeners personally and favorably. You may be speaking to a dozen people or an entire factory force, but the thrust to appeal to every individual is still of uppermost importance. Go quickly to your point and stay with it. They are probably all busy people, and they will have little patience if you cross the line between "all they want to know" to "more than they want to know." A direct, relaxed approach is always preferred in any business communication, because any sign of stress or confusion may be interpreted as slow thinking or a fundamental lack of knowledge.

This probably sounds far more basic than eloquent, which brings up the point that no matter how technical or detailed, your talk must never be dull.

Emerson wrote his recommendation for an eloquent speech — and, strange as it may seem to find it in the chapter on business, once you have considered it, you'll agree it is right where it belongs. He said:

"Come to the main matter of power of statement. Know your fact; hug your fact. For the essential thing is heat, and heat comes from sincerity. Speak what you know, and believe, and are personally in it. Eloquence is the power to translate the truth into language perfectly intelligible to the person to whom you speak."

For additional help in preparing your talk, consider these two aids. Pick up Theodore C. Sorensen's book, "Kennedy." It has some excellent information. Listen at every opportunity to good speakers. Analyze what they do — diagram their main points and the methods they used to make them powerful. Notice that, no matter how large the audience, they are talking to you.

## Show And Tell

It is best to refrain from using visual aids until you have had a good deal of experience. There are just too many chances for error if you are the least bit nervous. However, in a business talk, it is often essential that you incorporate some supportive material, so let us deal with it here. The following directions and precautions will help you to work smoothly with your equipment. There is no need to be afraid to try it if you prepare thoroughly.

First, and most important, keep in mind that whatever you are using, it is an *"aid."* It is not the speech itself. Many speakers start off well, but as soon as they pick up a pointer, or show a slide, they seem to think they have been dismissed. You, not the object being shown, are the animated one, and it is still up to you to hold attention.

Take into consideration, before electing to show slides, that it means the lights must be turned down and you will not be easily seen. It is, of course, much harder to keep contact with the audience when they are looking at something else. (Bring them back to you, from time to time, by asking a question.)

Arrive VERY early and test everything in sight. That includes the abilities of the person running the projector. You are on much safer ground if you can use a remote, so the slides change only when you want them to.

Never allow anyone else to do the commentary on your slides.

Be sure everyone can see. If using slides, it is best to have seats in a semi-circle, if possible. If you are using charts, they must be large; very large. Have the room set up and seating arrangement tested in advance to avoid the shifting of chairs and the atmosphere of home movies. Remain professional. Have an extra bulb with you. The one that is in the projector now is going to burn out. You should know at least the basic ways to repair the projector.

If you use diagrams or graphs, (they are more effective than a recitation of figures), they will be most impressive if they are in color — large and in bright colors.

If possible, arrange to have an over-head projector. There are several advantages. The lights can remain on. The slides are easily seen, and much lighter in weight if it's up to you to carry them. You can make your own transparencies and you can overlay on them.

Check and double check all your figures. It is somehow more unsettling to have someone rise up and point out a written error, still visible in bright, living color, than an oral one, gone into ether.

If you are going to use a pointer, don't pick it up before you are ready to use it, or your audience will race ahead of you and sit waiting for you to catch up.

If you are right-handed, take your pointer and walk to the left of the screen. If you cross your arm over your body to point, you will automatically turn your shoulder and head away from your audience, making it more difficult for them to see your face and follow your speech. When you point — point directly, don't wave around the general area.

Blackboard writing should be done ahead, if possible. Always write as little as possible, and it is far better not to do it at all.

Remember your audience and where they are. Look at them, not the chart. Some speakers become so engrossed in their graphs that the audience could tip toe back to their respective offices and never be missed.

It is best to give handouts well before or after your talk to avoid confusion and people trying to read when you want them to listen.

If you are going to be using aids, bring them to your speech class with you. If you are rehearsing a talk in class and say to the instructor, "Of course, when I give it to the members of the Rotary next week, I'll use slides so it will be better," she'll worry.

*Be fully prepared to give an excellent presentation without aids, should you find at the last moment that you will be unable to use them.*

If you carefully check through this chapter, and the

chapters on general rules for public speaking when you are preparing your talk, and again just before you present it — what can go wrong? Very little. You are well on your way to giving a splendid report, and being admired, even envied. If it is not exactly as you want it to be this time, just smile and say, "But watch me tomorrow. I'm going to be better every day!" The great thing is that you DID IT! You took an action. The others just sat and watched. Imagine, you're one of the people George Bernard Shaw was talking about when he said, "The people who get on in this world are the people who get up and look for the circumstances they want, and if they can't find them, they make them." (You're pretty good, when George Bernard Shaw notices you.)

# Chapter Seven

## How Do You Look On The Phone?

It would be impossible to write on the importance of a rich, vibrant speaking voice without including some comments about its importance in a telephone conversation. On the phone, as on the radio, your voice stands unadorned to establish your individual personality and even to create in the subconscious mind of the listener a picture of your physical appearance. How often have you had an occasion to speak with someone several times on the phone before actually meeting her in person and then found yourself saying, "I somehow thought she would be older," or, "I thought she would look quite different." You may have conceived the person as being heavy or very thin and you may find yourself surprised that she "doesn't look like her voice."

It is important to put some thought and time in on this phase of your day. Those master statisticians in the telephone company tell us that the average person, between home and office, spends 365 hours a year on the telephone. Anything you spend that much time doing is worth doing well.

Your home phone can serve as an excellent instrument for improving your voice. Nowhere is it easier to check your speaking habits and patterns and to make corrections. Here are just a few suggestions you will be able to incorporate into your schedule without involving extra time in your busy day.

Place a mirror on the wall near your home phone (never a mirror in your office) and use it occasionally to watch yourself as you speak. Are you articulating well — using your tongue, lips and jaws — or is it sometimes difficult to discern visibly when you are listening and when you have picked up the conversation? This is a great time to overexaggerate if you find you are guilty of muttering. How often are you asked to repeat when placing an order over the phone? That is usually an indication that you have become a victim of lazy speech habits rather than a problem of volume and it is time to start practicing the articulation drills in the chapter entitled, "Speech Class for One."

It is also a wise policy when conducting a business call and giving a name and address to insure that sounds easily confused are correctly heard by simply making it a habit to say, "Please send that order to Ms. Marion Finard, that is F as in Frank, i-n-a-r-d."

Did you know that a pencil kept by the phone should not be used only for jotting down messages? It can also make a decided improvement in your voice? Just hold it down about eight inches below the mouthpiece and talk down to it. It will automatically lower the pitch of your voice, bringing it into the deeper, fuller tones that are more flattering. It will also help you to attain the correct volume so that your conversation is more comfortable to listen to at the other end of the line.

## Why Are You Shouting?

For some reason that has never been clearly defined, most people feel it is part of their duty in life to aid the telephone company, especially with long distance calls, by shouting. If not by an actual shout at least with the most booming voice they can muster. Perhaps it is just a common tendency to try whenever possible to be helpful. In this case, the telephone company will assure you that shouting is not helpful, and is never necessary, even on international calls. It is still, however, a capital idea to speak up. We may be unaware of a distracting background noise at the listener's end of the line which makes it difficult for her to hear accurately. While the telephone focuses the caller's voice directly into the listener's ear, she does not have the visual aid of watching the speaker's expressions and that tends often to make it a bit harder to hear. The best way to aid "Ma Bell" is by employing your most precise articulation.

## Your Tape Recorder

Beside your phone is definitely the place to keep your tape recorder. When you pick up the receiver, switch the recorder on and record your own part of the conversation. Never record the other party unless she has specifically asked you to do so. Even if it is a very close friend or relative and you are simply doing it for fun, it will be considered a poor joke and indeed it would be in bad taste. (Incidentally, it is also illegal.)

But *your* taped conversation can be helpful beyond measure. Perhaps the first few times you will be too aware of the recording to talk in your natural pattern, but sooner or later someone will ring and you will become engrossed in such an interesting conversation that the recorder will slip your mind completely, and that is the time you will want to play it back, perhaps several times. Now you can catch the "and a's" in all their glory — you will listen to the repeated phrases you never hear yourself say, such as, "no kidding?", "O.K.", "right!", "wow", "well, at this point in time", "feedback" and the very common, "you know." Now, Ms., you can really roll up your sleeves and start to work on your speech patterns and rid yourself of those troublesome speech tics that creep into your conversations so effortlessly that you are not even aware they have invaded.

## Speech Tics

Those persistent words and phrases which are repeated by some persons over and over again have become commonly known as Speech Tics. While they are as clear and as abrasive as a fingernail on a blackboard to the listener, they are seldom even heard by the person using them. It is this very unawareness which makes them so difficult to eliminate.

A prominent businessman had acquired the bad habit of swearing. It became so natural to him that finally his simplest sentences included at least one unnecessary word. One day while he was telling a story his wife asked, "Couldn't you explain that to us without swearing"? The man, with an expression of complete bewilderment and confusion, answered, "Who the hell is swearing"?

Some speech tics are common and probably adopted unconsciously by hearing them used so often by others. Some you may find are uniquely your own.

A woman married many years irritated her friends unknowingly by confirming everything she said by asking her husband, "Isn't that right, Harry"? As simple a statement as, "It's a beautiful day"! grew into, "It's a beautiful day, isn't it Harry"? When someone once asked her why she felt it was necessary to check every word with Harry, she was indignant. "I never ask him anything," she said, "I have a strong mind of my own and I always say exactly the way I feel about matters, don't I Harry"?

The very first step in overcoming a Speech Tic is to hear it yourself. You will find your tape recorder an excellent helper. Listen to it carefully.

Ask someone else if she can tell you a word or phrase that you use repeatedly. It may be best to ask this of someone in your office or in an organization to which you belong socially, as often those within a family tend to develop the same speech tendencies or block out the redundant phrases of other family members. Ask someone to count for you the number of times you use your particular word in an evening. The number may astound you.

Once you have isolated your problem, listen for that word or phrase every time you talk. If you hear it you can begin to make a lasting correction by using one of two methods.

You may stop abruptly each time you hear yourself using that pattern and repeat the sentence precisely without it —

"I expect to leave on Thursday, you know."
STOP! REPEAT!
"I expect to leave on Thursday."

It's a nuisance and a bother to correct it each time. Of course it is, but it is well worth doing for a week or two, and far less annoying than a lifetime of "you knows."

A second method also takes an extra moment of time, but it is time well spent. Lengthen the phrase and force yourself to say the entire phrase every time you hear yourself starting it.

"I expect to leave on Thursday, you know- -CONTINUE (you know) exactly what my meaning is, I'm sure, but if you have any question, please ask me."

You will soon tire of that amount of extra explaining and you will annoy yourself as much as you have been annoying others in the past. Your mind will soon race ahead to that troublesome phrase and you will be able to consciously stop before uttering it. Either method will work, but the one chosen must be done consistently.

### Telephone Manners

This is an ideal time to review telephone manners. If you are placing the call, be sure you allow at least ten rings. It takes that many rings to give the person one minute to answer the call. If you wish to speak to someone enough to take the time and trouble to dial, then permit her enough time to answer her phone. Most people have several phones at convenient places, but it is still possible she is in the yard, deep in the storeroom, or just stepping out of the shower as the first ring sounds. Few things are as frustrating as making a dash for the telephone and arriving just in time to hear someone click off on the third ring. (Chances are she will call you back later and start off the conversation with, "It's so hard to reach you; you're never home"! That salutation is seldom appreciated and best left unsaid.)

If the call is answered by someone in the house, other than the person to whom you wish to speak, it is thoughtful to say, "Hello" and give your name. As long as the person has taken the trouble to answer the phone and to assist you, she deserves a bit more courtesy than an abrupt, "Is Susan there"?

Once you have reached your party, if you wish to discuss something at length or to visit for more than a minute, make it a point to ask if it is a convenient time or whether it would be better if you called back later. Many a dinner has grown cold, and many a dinner partner grown furious while someone else holds up a meal with a thoughtlessly unnecessary conversation. If you start by saying you wish to speak with her for only a minute, then remember what you said and limit the call. Just for the record, it is still proper in social conversations for the person who placed the call to end it.

Many people resent stating who they are when phoning a business office, a doctor or lawyer with whom they wish to discuss a personal matter, but it is a fair question for the receptionist to ask. Often it will save you time as well as making it easier for the person you are calling if you identify yourself. Most receptionists are instructed to ask the name of the caller.

If you are answering a business phone and the person asked for is not available at that time, it is considerate to state that fact first and then ask, "May I ask who is calling"? If you reverse this procedure it may leave the party who placed the call unnecessarily uncomfortable.

If you are placing a business call it is wise to jot down the points to be covered first. If the person on the other end of the line diverts the conversation it is easy to neglect some information that was pertinent. It weakens your image of efficiency if you must call back frequently to say, "I forgot to tell you the meeting is at 2:00 and your report will be first on the agenda."

When calling even the closest of friends it is still best to give your name since several of her acquaintances may have similar voices on the phone. A call that starts with, "Bet you can't guess who this is"? gives you a major clue immediately. It is someone you know with a juvenile mentality.

Regardless of which end of the line you are on, never attempt to talk while munching away on food, smoking a cigarette, or heaven forbid, chewing gum!

One final word before you hang up. If you think that because the other person cannot see you she can't tell if she has disturbed you, awakened you or interrupted your favorite television program, you're wrong. Your voice will tell her loud and clear if you are not careful, and it will be more convincing than any denials you may futilely attempt to make.

Is it really possible for someone to tell whether or not you smile on the phone? If you don't believe it, try and "*see*"!

# Chapter Eight

## Overcoming Submissive Speech

Much has been said and written over the past few years about Feminine Speech. It has come to mean any expression which is inserted to qualify a statement, apologize unnecessarily, add a self-answering question or supply the speaker with two "exit doors", one from which she may later deny what she said and the other by which she may modify her original meaning. It is a highly undesirable form of speech and blatantly belies the positive thinking woman. For example:
"If you're not too busy I'd sorta like to have this report typed-up by tonight."
Does she want it typed today or not? If it isn't done because the impression she gave was that it wasn't an important matter, will she say the next day, "I asked to have this report typed up by last night and today it is still sitting here and not done."
For women who direct, instruct or hold authority, Feminine Speech is a serious detriment. Many women, still perhaps feeling a bit uncomfortable with their new status, try to minimize their role to make those in lesser positions feel more comfortable by softening their instructions in this manner. It is seldom effective and rarely a kindness. Rather than show comradeship, it is more apt to create an image of insecurity.
Showing the new office employee the daily procedures, a newly appointed supervisor may say, "We sorta

do it this way." The new girl on the floor had better not "sorta" do it any other way. The way it has been done is the way it is to be done — but she wasn't exactly told that.

Most women are trying to show that they are not gloating in their new power; they are still humble. They are constantly trying to reassure others that they are compatible and approachable. While this intention is admirable, their error is in the manner in which they are attempting to do it. It is by the tone of voice and the pleasant firmness of their speech that they will communicate an empathy with their subordinates while maintaining their status. A slightly deeper tone of authority and a smile with a 'thank you' will accomplish far more.

Sometimes this pattern of speech is not strictly limited to women, but it is proposed to be the speech of those without power in both sexes. It is not indicative of only those without power, but it is embraced also by those uncomfortable with authority, and the definition should be expanded to include them. It is predominately found in women, but not exclusively.

Consider a few examples. Do you ever find yourself inclined to use this apologetic speech pattern when you are speaking socially with men who intimidate you? How about with superiors in your office? Do you use it with other women who you feel are on a higher social and financial plane? At times are you aware of other women using this form of speech?

\* \* \* \* \*

- *Well, maybe* we *could* ask Mrs. Stevens for some help on this project.

Instead, why not state,

- We shall ask Mrs. Stevens to clarify the procedures she wants used in this project.

\* \* \* \* \*

- It's *really super* hard to face an audience, but I *guess* I'll *probably* have to do it.

Try it this way:
- It is hard to face an audience, but I'll do it.

\* \* \* \* \*

- I *suppose* it's *awfully* soon to ask for another increase in the budget, *but if it's all right with you* I *really* think . . .

If you cannot operate without the increase try:
- It is absolutely essential to increase the budget at this time.

\* \* \* \* \*

- We've been waiting for a long time, *haven't we?*

After an hour that question, if voiced at all, should have been a concrete statement.

\* \* \* \* \*

- Mt. St. Helen's was *really sort of* a big natural wonder, *wasn't it?*

Sure was!

\* \* \* \* \*

- *I know I've only been here three months, which is really kind of a short time, so maybe I shouldn't even mention this, but I was wondering if it isn't too much trouble, etc., etc.* . . .

(If she ever did reach the point, she forgot it. It was all right because the others had stopped listening anyway.)

\* \* \* \* \*

Any "golly" or "gee whiz" statement made anywhere at any time should be eliminated. (*Well, maybe* if the fellow you're *really* trying *awfully* hard to *kinda* impress hits a bull's eye from 60 feet, one breathy "*gee whiz —* that was *really terrific*", might accomplish something.)

You have no reason to put yourself down so don't do it; nor do you need to be abrasive or arrogant to gain attention. You need only to take the time to weigh what you have to say in terms of your knowledge and its value, and present it in a straight forward, convincing manner with a pleasingly confident tone. Evaluate yourself, then strive to improve, but do not ever deny or apologize for your worth.

DeBalzac said it well for all times. "Nothing is a greater impediment to being on good terms with others, than being ill at ease with yourself."

If you have merited a position of authority — have studied a subject and are knowledgeable about it — have had experience enough with an issue to draw a conclusion, or you have read enough to have formed a reasonable opinion, state it. Do it with tact and consideration, but without endless qualification. You do not have to be a radical feminist to want people to recognize your abilities and respect your opinions. Drop "rather," "sort of," "kinda," "awfully," "very," "really" and "dumb isn'it it"? today.

Do not kinda guess that, if it's O.K. with everyone, maybe enough has been said about Feminine Speech. You know enough has been said.

# Chapter Nine

## Don't Allow Your Voice To Be Older Than You Are!

One of the most appealing aspects of developing better speech is that with every goal you reach, you are rewarded with a number of additional benefits. If you practice the breathing exercises in this chapter, not only will you gain additional resonance in your voice, but you will also sound youthful and more vital. There are other exciting improvements you will notice, also. Correct breathing promotes better health, improves poor posture, complements personal appearance, and gives a lift to your attitudes and general well-being. These are all pluses!

The greatest profits for you will result from the exercises done primarily to strengthen and rejuvenate your voice, because they are the ones that establish proper breathing habits. If you are curious as to the extent that daily pressures and tension can tighten your voice, here's an easy way to feel how rigid your throat muscles can become and how high and strained they may force your voice to sound.

Place your hands on your throat. Now, whisper the following jingle.

My voice should be relaxed and clear,
Confident, pleasing and easy to hear!

You should not feel any vibration at all with your fingers. (If you do, you are one of the many people who find they do not really whisper. They lower their voices, but do not cease to use their vocal chords. Practice just blowing your breath out — then blow one word, starting with a wh sound — when, where, why. Try other words starting with H, P, or F until you can combine several words together without employing your vocal chords.)

Now say the jingle out loud and you will feel your voice come into play by the vibrating on your fingers. Your throat should still be relaxed.

This time try the same lines, but scream them out. Scream, really scream as though you had the lead in a horror movie and this is the climax scene.

Feel how strained your throat muscles become. Listen to the shrillness in your voice. It is exaggerated tension. Daily pressures to a lesser degree cause that same tightness, and without realizing it your voice creeps a tone higher and becomes less attractive and more strident to those who must listen to it. In the chapter "A Speech Class For One," you practiced relaxing your throat and opening the passageway. Now you will be able to reinforce your deeper tones with a stronger breath.

The person who incorporates full diaphragm breathing into her daily life not only speaks with more impressive tones, but also appears slimmer, has a more attractive bust line, tends to have less illness, sleeps more soundly and in general has greater endurance than her shallow-breathing peers. Isn't that worth the forming of a good habit? Try these simple daily exercises and you will be delighted with the noticeable results.

The best way to begin is with a simple self-check to be sure you know precisely the area of your diaphragm which is the base for your breath support.

Lie flat on your back with your hands on your rib cage, (one high, just below your breasts and the other touching just below that hand). Now simulate a cough. This simple procedure lets you feel exactly the area you want to engage in your breathing program. No tummy breathing allowed. Your stomach muscles should be firm, forming a natural girdle, so pull them in. To be sure those muscles are tight, try grunting and you will feel them working.

Now take several deep breaths and feel the movement under your hands as your diaphragm expands and contracts. Breathe through your nose, not through your mouth.

When you are sure that you are breathing correctly from your diaphragm, try the same procedure in a standing position.

Be sure to stand straight, shoulders back and feet just a little way apart for good balance. Keep your tummy muscles tightened. Hold your hands over your diaphragm as before and take several deep breaths through your nose. Again, you will feel the expanding and contracting when you are breathing correctly.

Next, using any vowel sound, see how long you can sustain it while exhaling after a full breath through your nose. (You will not have to be concerned about doing this while inhaling, as it is impossible to talk while you are inhaling. If you had not realized this before, exhale your breath until your lungs are empty and while inhaling again try to say, "I am speaking." Now back to what you should be doing.)

Try: aaaaaaaaaaa or eeeeeeeeee, or your doctor's favorite — ahahahahahahah.

Try it again, this time counting to yourself as you project the vowel sound. You should reach 20 quite easily. If you are in fine physical condition you should have no trouble reaching 50.

While removing one hand from your diaphragm, hold your index finger about six inches away from your lips. Through your nose take a normal breath, releasing it now in a controlled, steady stream. Feel your breath completely empty from your body. Repeat this exercise again and count to yourself, going as far beyond 20 as possible. You should not be satisfied until you count to 50, and if you practice daily, or when possible several times during each day, you will find it will not be long before you discover distinct improvement. If 50 is beyond your ability now, keep practicing until you can comfortably reach that goal. It is said when Napoleon was asked the single most essential ingredient of success he said, "Practice." It still applies to everything you wish to do well, whether it's dancing, tennis, needlepoint, golf or speaking.

If you will try these deep-breathing exercises before going to bed, you'll notice that even on nights when you are overtired you will fall asleep more easily, and each day your voice will be fuller, with more resonance. If you are nervous when traveling by plane, especially when your flight takes off, or is about to land, or if you feel vaguely upset or nauseous at any time, these slow, deep-breathing exercises will help.

Professor Kenney of Emerson College credited over 40 years of teaching without missing a day because of illness, or ever having suffered from a single common cold, solely to a regime of simple deep-breathing exercises practiced daily, often while walking to work. His tones had the depth and strength of a young man's voice even in his advanced years.

Only the very, very young want to be told, "Oh, you sounded so much older on the phone, I'm surprised. You are much younger than I thought you would be." If we are going to work to maintain a more youthful appearance, we must never belie it with a tired, restricted voice. Rather, why not paraphrase Murphy's law and promise, "If there is anything (about me) that can be improved, I'll improve it."

At which point in your life should you begin to think about the resonance of your voice? As in all areas of improvement, now is the time to start. Certain cosmetic concerns used to advertise, "Under 30 protect, over 30 preserve." It is unfortunate there are no commercials for the tender, loving care of our voices, but if there were they would unanimously proclaim this one message — "Cultivate carefully forever!" Such advertisements could also offer us an abundance of coupons for a bounty of health-filled bonuses.

## Careless Speech Habits

>To slur is human —
>to enunciate divine

Although slurred speech is not only a weakness of adults, it is perhaps even more inexcusable among mature, established men and women. United States natives are the fastest speaking people in the world. Someone said our strongest national characteristic is that we are always in a hurry. This, unfortunately, overflows into our speech and is responsible for the slurring of many simple words.

This is an excellent time to bring your tape recorder out and check the troublesome small words you may slide over. Here are just a few to listen for as you play back a recorded conversation.

Do you say —
- ken for can?
- ya for you?
- ta for to?
- jest for just?
- fer for for?
- git for get?

Ken I jest git some groceries fer ya ta take home?
or, how about —

May I just buy some groceries for you to take home?

There is a long list of commonly slurred words and phrases and as you become more acutely aware of speech patterns you will hear them quite readily. You will find it challenging to add your own discoveries to this starter list, and you'll be surprised at how fast your list will grow. Have you heard —

    dja for did you?
    iny for any?
    I wanna for I want to?
    meetcha for meet you?
    wile for while?
    pitcher for picture?
    histry for history?
    bekuz for because?
    goverment for government?
    outta for ought to?
    lemme for let me?
    idear for idea?

And please, women of America, unite and:
    Let's lay to rest the "des" and "does"
    Beneath the headstone of "ya knows".

It is interesting to notice how often a person who would never consider wearing the same outfit for two consecutive days, will employ the same worn out, colorless words in her conversation. Your speech should be reviewed and updated as conscientiously as your wardrobe. Tasteful originality is as refreshing in your speech as in your dress.

There are six hundred thousand words in our language, but the average business person uses less than three thousand. Never attempt to flaunt your vocabulary. An ostentatious conversation is as unbecoming as gaudy jewelry. However, a little sparkle can perk up your image and be achieved by selecting familiar words that give a more precise meaning. How many words can you substitute for the overworked — awful or good?

    The play was (good)   The play was (awful)
    entertaining, potent,    dull, listless,
    amusing, meaningful  lengthy, amateurish

Slang, unless it is extremely clever or serves a definite purpose, discredits the person who uses it, and has no rightful place in your "wardrobe of words."

# Chapter Ten

## Being Shy Is Not an Excuse

Do you know people who use the excuse that they are shy for not taking part in any project where they would have to stand up and express themselves? Sometimes, they seem to flaunt shyness, proudly announcing it as though it were an honorary title. It is not. Of course, everyone is hesitant to some degree, but if you are waiting for a day to dawn when you will suddenly feel completely self-assured, confident, witty, authoritative and eager to meet challenges head on — unless it is a false courage — that day will probably never come.

It is, of course, much easier to let the other person speak up, and to stay safely out of the line of fire. But it is difficult to accomplish anything from the sidelines, and the reward for all that security and escape is mediocrity. The only person, it is said, who has never been criticized, is the person who has never done anything. Certainly, we all have some worth to offer. Perhaps the saddest of all epitaphs was written anonymously:

> His life went on from day to day,
> For him it held no terrors —
> St. Peter wrote the final score —
> No hits — no runs — no errors!

We all hope for something a little more impressive than

a final report which reads like that. It is not an easy thing to put a lifetime of feeling shy and unsure behind you, but it can be done.

## Social Shyness

To overcome shyness in social situations, there is probably no better method than the one President Roosevelt said he used for years. He explained that as a young man, it was most difficult for him to feel at ease meeting new people, until he determined that the other person was feeling a bit reluctant, also. Consequently, he promised himself he would spend the first three minutes with each new acquaintance trying to help her overcome her shyness. It worked. He transferred his feeling of shyness away from himself and thought of it as someone else's problem. It was then much easier for him to deal with his own insecurity. It helps to remember what a wise professor once told his class, "The biggest sound in the word SHY is I. If you eliminate that sound, the rest is just a breath of air that floats away."

## Too Shy to Speak Out

One of the main obstacles to speaking before a group is that there is no place to practice. Standing in front of the mirror in your bedroom is really not at all the same as facing a hundred people from behind a rostrum. Sports teams can practice together before they run onto the field or court; actors and vocalists have plenty of rehearsal time prior to a performance; but the poor guest speaker is suddenly just "there."

That is not quite true, or it needn't be. There are many smaller steps that are most effective that you can take before the day when you stand and present your new idea to the Board of Directors. The most obvious, of course, is to enroll in a speech or public speaking course. If you never speak in public, it will still help you to gain self-confidence and to become a more discriminating listener. (See chapter on "Why You Should Study Public Speaking If You Are Never Going To Speak In Public.")

If you cannot work a Continuing Education class into your schedule, be alert for other every day "rehearsal times."

When you arrive at a meeting and the chairman says, "Our secretary has been called out of town today; I wonder if I may have a volunteer to read her report?" That is the time for you to raise your hand and say "Yes." It has all been written out for you. Everyone knows you are doing it on short notice; she will not criticize a thing, because she is so grateful that she has not been drafted for the job.

### The Sunday Service Reader

If your church is looking for additional readers, speak out, say "Yes" and sign up. Just for starters you'll have the greatest material that has ever been written! Be sure to make the most of this opportunity. It would be wise for you to spend a little time preparing for this reading, if you want to feel as comfortable as possible, and to present the material effectively. Be sure to pick up a copy and bring it home with you several days in advance. Always familiarize yourself thoroughly with whatever material you will be using in any situation. To simply look it over before the service that morning can produce something akin to disaster. Plan to read the section you have been assigned *out loud* several times. Words and phrases sound much differently to the ear when they are voiced than you imagine they sound when you read silently. Also, you will want to check on the pronunciation of Biblical names; if you find a word troublesome, write it lightly in pencil on the margin as it sounds when you pronounce it. You can invent your own phonetic guidelines — whatever is easiest for you.

Underlining words you wish to stress, and placing a vertical line where you wish to pause will help with your phrasing, especially if you are inclined to read a bit too fast.

> "*Therefore*/I *say* unto *you*/take *no* thought for your *life*/*what* you shall *eat*/or *what* you shall *drink*/nor yet for your *body*/*what* you shall *put on.*/Is *not* the *life* more than *meat*/ and the *body more* than *raiment?*
>
> (Matthew 6.)

Your voice should clearly indicate the end of a sentence and the final words of a reading. The listener should realize when you have finished.

The first few Sundays you may find yourself holding tight to the book, scared to death to look up, but someday you'll accidentally glance at someone in the first pew and discover that she is looking at you with approving interest. She may even smile. Look again the following week. The situation is improving. Now your grip is not quite so tight on the book, and your voice has come down almost a full octave, you have stopped shaking, and minor miracle — you're looking up at the congregation and enjoying it! You may receive no crown in heaven for this effort, because your profits will be so great right here on earth.

If you are fortunate enough to have children in your home, or in your neighborhood, try gathering a small group together for some story telling. You can start by reading old favorites, and then, little by little, try a short tale without the book. You'll find you have a great audience, and chances are you'll have practice with as animated a question period as you will ever encounter.

Best of all, if you can take a few minutes to visit a local nursing home and volunteer to spend a little time each month reading the favorite poems of yesterday to a group of elderly residents, I will guarantee that you will never find a more appreciative and enthusiastic audience. Seldom will you ever be able to give more joy, or receive richer rewards!

Don't expect too much from yourself; be prepared to make a few mistakes along the way. Everyone does. Don't set the standards for yourself higher than you would set them for others. If everyone stopped at her first mistake, no one would move ahead. Then, learn to evaluate criticism. If it is constructive, pay close attention and learn how you can improve. If it is simply petty, ignore it. Nobel prizes would not be awarded, nor Oscars presented, if the first bad review had stopped the artists. (However, you can be sure it wounded them a little, but they recovered; so will you.) Don't ever be intimidated by the fear that relatives, friends or co-workers may ask, "Why is she doing that," or "Who does she think she is?" You think you are a fairly intelligent, capable person, and you are about to prove it. Given a little time and allowance for a couple of errors, you will. It is always better to be the person accomplishing something than the one criticizing. Those criticizing may even learn from you someday.

Don't allow yourself to go through life filled with needless fears. Ask yourself, is it necessary to fear criticism from others? Is it wise to fear the opinions of others, or has it just become a habit you haven't stopped to realize? Are foolish fears standing in the way of your abilities and efforts to establish the self-confidence you need? Are you allowing a fear of others to stop you from speaking up and striving to speak effectively? Why should you allow anyone to thwart your progress and hold a negative control over your life? Don't ever allow your greatest lack to be your own inability to speak out. You can contribute your worth and increase your accomplishments once you determine to conquer worthless fears. It takes a bit of commitment and a slice of personal courage, but the first time you know you have presented your ideas with clarity, and someone says to you, "You speak with such poise and confidence, it's a pleasure to listen to you," you will know the results are truly worth the effort.

# Chapter Eleven

## How To Introduce A Speaker

If you have never spoken before a formal audience, here is the perfect assignment for you! It is relatively easy and takes very little time on the platform, while offering numerous rewards. You will have a mini-public speaking opportunity, visibility, a chance to prove to yourself that you can handle additional responsibility and, most important of all, you will face an audience, speak effectively and successfully, and find that you can enjoy it. All these benefits for simply standing up and introducing a speaker. It is not difficult. It is a position in which it is almost impossible to fail, unless you give it no previous thought at all. The woman who introduced an author by saying, "We are all looking forward to his new book, and hope it will be an all time best seller, as his last two novels were so poorly received," needed a good deal of additional preparation. This could never happen to you, because you can refer to and follow these simple guidelines.

### How To Prepare

There is very little research work involved in preparing the introduction you are to give. The one essential step is to contact the speaker, either by mail or phone, and ask her to supply you with a résumé relevant to the talk she will be presenting, and all the additional material she would like included in her introduction. Speakers are always ready to supply introduction material. If you simply adhere to the material they give you, there is very little chance for error. You may wish to enhance it a bit and add a complimentary comment, but basically your work of preparation will be done for you. You will most certainly please the speaker if you follow her guidelines.

It is always acceptable to add a sincere compliment, but the superlatives should not be effusive to the point that they become embarrassing. There is an often quoted story of a speaker who listened to one enthusiastic exclamation of flattery after another, until he became uneasy. When he finally reached the podium, he announced, "After listening to that introduction, I can hardly wait to hear what I have to say!"

## At The Podium

All of the elements that are present in any form of public speaking pertain to making introductions. Be sure you read and incorporate all the suggestions in the chapter, "You Too Can Survive Being The Guest Speaker," because they are of equal importance to you. Think, too, about your voice and the importance of a relaxed, open throat and the lower tones you need to give an impressive introduction. In addition, here are a few suggestions that are uniquely pertinent to your particular talk.

- Be sure that you are pronouncing the speaker's name correctly. If you have the slightest doubt, check it out and write it on your cue card as it sounds, rather than the way it is spelled.
- If the speaker has supplied you with a title to her talk, be sure you include that, as well as the subject matter.
- Do arrive early enough to meet and talk with the guest speaker before the meeting. Thank her for the material she sent to you, and ask if there is anything else she would like to add. Double check your facts

with her so that she does not have to start her speech with a correction. If you are including any facts taken from the newspaper, check them with her for accuracy.
- No matter how certain you are that you will remember the speaker's name and the title of her talk, write them both on your cue card, but do not read them unless absolutely necessary. That is simply back-up insurance.
- While it is complimentary to point out the interest there is in the speaker's subject, remember that it is her talk, and refrain from presenting it for her. An introduction should seldom take more than two or three minutes. You will be surprised at how much you can say about the speaker, her subject, and her background in that length of time.
- You should look at the audience and not at the speaker until turning to her at the end of the introduction, when her name is announced or repeated.
- Check with the speaker regarding a question period. If there is to be time at the end of her talk for questions, you should include that information in your introduction.
- You may join in the applause when you finish, as it is directed to the speaker, not to you.
- When presenting the speaker's background, you should include all the material that qualifies her to speak on the subject she has chosen and omit superfluous data.
- Remember your purpose is to interest the audience in hearing the speaker — to point out to them why this topic is of timely importance to them, and why this particular speaker is eminently qualified to speak on it — and to create a friendly atmosphere of anticipation.

story or anecdote about the speaker or her subject which will help to set the stage, that is excellent, as long as you do not prolong it beyond the few minutes allotted to you.
- If you have come on to the stage to make the introduction, it is best to return to the audience when the speaker reaches the podium, rather than to remain seated on stage.
- When the speaker has finished, it is your responsibility to thank her briefly and either adjourn the meeting or turn it back to the chairman.
- Try to avoid the stale, stilted opening statements, such as, "It is my privilege . . . We are honored tonight . . . It is with the greatest of pleasure . . . etc."

The guest speaker may or may not accomplish her end of persuading, entertaining, informing or gaining an endorsement. But if you have addressed your first audience, you have taken an upward step in establishing your own confidence and self worth. You have proven to yourself that you can do it. For you, it has been a most successful day!

# Chapter Twelve

## You Too Can Be A Guest Speaker

She was speaking from her seat in a speech class. She was explaining that she had enrolled in the class because she was determined that she would overcome her fear of facing an audience, but she would have to do it her own way. She wanted to break it up into parts: Part one — to stand up; Part two would be walking to the podium, and Part three would be facing the audience.

All her classmates encouraged her to do it in the most comfortable way for her and assured her they were all there to back her up.

Several weeks later, she was as far as the podium, but she stood there with her back to the class. "I do want to address you," she said, "but I just don't feel that I want to face you yet." The class strained to hear her as she spoke into the wall, but they were encouraging, sympathetic and patient. Two more weeks passed, but then it happened! With a look of steel determination, she walked again to the front of the room, remembered to turn at the podium, gave the class an expression they were sure was meant to be a smile, and with hands shaking only slightly and clenching huge cue cards, she delivered a three line speech with hardly a mistake! Never did 25 women applaud more loudly. It was the enthusiastic kind of ovation for which most public speakers would sell their souls! She smiled, relaxed and said, "Thank you," with the confidence of a pro! It was a great night. She had conquered those overpowering nerves.

If those same nerves have kept you seated in the background, restricted you from showing your abilities and sharing your ideas, then the following pages are for you!

## Nerves — You Can Control Them!

Petrified! That is the most commonly used word to describe the feeling most women (and men, too) have when asked to stand and address a group for the first time. If you think you could never overcome it, that speaking up and speaking out is just impossible for you, read on. If you have already tried speaking before a group and shook every minute you were on the stage, read on.

If you are going to progress you must be able to stand on your feet and express yourself. You may not need to face an audience of thousands, but presenting a report, introducing a guest speaker, explaining policies and procedures to new employees, making a suggestion for raising money for church activities, or any other occasion where you stand and speak to a group of people, is a Public Speaking Situation. You must be able to take control, face your audience and speak out effectively. If your nerves rule you, they need to be brought into line, and now is the time to do it.

Everyone who must face an audience feels apprehension, no matter how often she has done it. Each group is different and each time is a brand new time. Joan Rivers, Shirley Chisholm, Barbara Walters — all admit freely that they are still nervous before making an appearance. All good speakers will tell you the same thing. How do they do it time after time and thrive on it to the point of enjoyment? They all do exactly the same thing.

They make their nerves work for them to enhance, rather than detract from, what they are doing. How? They channel those shaky feelings into enthusiasm. They harness that nervousness by telling themselves, "I'm excited — I'm excited because this is going to be a great audience — They are going to respond to everything I tell them — I've got the best material I've ever had and this is going to be one terrific speech — I can't wait to get started!" When a good speaker walks to the podium, she is not thinking I-I-I — she is thinking "we." OK audience, "we" are going to communicate. You are anxious to hear what I have to tell you, and I am convinced you will be as enthusiastic about it as I am! You were great to invite me, and I am as excited as I can be about being here with you! She is saying it inside and the audience knows it by the way she walks to the podium, the way she thanks the person who introduced her, and the way that she smiles and greets them. They are supportive of her, even before she begins to speak.

How do you go from a "near collapse" to a "can't wait to get started" state of mind? You do it thoughtfully, thoroughly and purposefully, until you have reasoned and disciplined yourself to reach that goal. Try it.

Start by analyzing exactly what it is that you fear. (You and just about everyone else in the world. According to a poll taken by the London Sunday Times, asking people to list their ten greatest fears, speaking before a group was number one by 41%, followed by heights, insects and only then, financial problems.) If you are to overcome it, you must look at it as objectively as you would a sore throat, and deal with it. Here are the three culprits that most often are responsible for those shaky knees.

I. Fear of being stared at. Strange as that may sound to you at first, most people do not like others looking directly at them for a long period of time. They unconsciously feel that those who are staring are criticizing. Some offer the theory that it is a throwback to prehistoric days. Animals will usually circle and stare at each other before attacking. It is an uncomfortable position for most people, but it has no validity in this situation. Unless you are jumping right into the middle of a controversy or politics (and neither would be a wise move for a fledgling public speaker) you will not be facing a hostile audience. They have come because they are interested and want to hear what you have to say. Not a single person there is hoping that you will fail. When did you ever sit in an audience, hoping a disaster would overtake the speaker? No one does. If you look directly at an audience, and especially if you take just a moment to smile at them, you will notice that everyone there will smile back at you. Some groups are more difficult to face than others, and strangely enough, the people who make you the most nervous are apt to be your relatives, your in-laws and your peers. Strangers comprise the easiest audience to address. Ask yourself, now, do I need to fear people looking at me? Am I nervous when talking with one person? Two? Then why ten, fifteen or twenty? They are looking at you in pairs of two — look directly back at them in the same way — plan to speak with them as individuals. Start now to notice the attitudes and behaviours of the next speakers to whom you listen. Analyze the manner in which they approach the audience. No matter how large the audience, good speakers give the impression that they are speaking to you personally, and mentally that is exactly what they are doing. They are talking to *you*, sharing something they are knowledgeable about with *you*, and they want *you* to appreciate it with them. Audiences — individuals, are sensitive to your feelings, so try not to make them tense. Relax with them. Think about it. Make up your mind that you will greet your audience as you would a group of friends coming into your home. They have taken off their coats and have been seated; now is it really so difficult to visit with them and tell them the news?

II. Fear of looking foolish. Well, you could trip walking to the podium, you could drop your cue cards, you could sneeze and lose your place, you might find the mike has gone dead, or your stocking has a run, or, perhaps, you might even tip over the glass of water. Maybe there are other things that might go wrong, but they all fall a little short of a natural disaster. If you don't make an issue of an upset, no one else will. If you trip, a smile and a laugh will relax your audience as well as yourself. A *very* short "excuse me" dismisses a cough or sneeze. If your mouth goes dry, a quick bite on your tongue will take care of it nicely, and the next time you'll remember to have a lifesaver or lozenges to place between your teeth and cheek before you speak. (Never to chew on while you're talking!) If you reason it out a bit, you are more apt to have something happen which will delay you in reaching the meeting on time, than having any catastrophe once you've arrived on stage. If you are not a ridiculous person, and you do not make yourself appear ridiculous, the audience certainly will not think you are. They will enjoy your talk and forgive your mistakes if you make them laugh with you, but they will never ridicule you because of an accident or error.

III. Fear of going blank. This needless worry you can dismiss at once. That is not to say it cannot and does not happen, but rather that you can arrange for any such eventuality ahead of time and defeat it long before it has a chance to attack you. First, never memorize your speech. NEVER! Outline it, practice it, review it until you have your facts set firmly in place, but don't ever write it out word for word and memorize it. (If it is to be published, or copies given to the press, that is something different. Most of the speeches in that category are read and that is beyond the initial steps we are concerned with here.) Once you have refined your outline, make up your cue cards following these guidelines carefully.

- Always use cards, never paper. It is too flimsy to handle easily and it is noisy if you are using a mike.
- Print the cards in large lettering so that you can pick up your thought at a glance. (Print, do not write, as printing is much easier to read quickly.)
- Use several different colored felt point pens to make it easier to find your place.
- Put very little printing on each card to allow for several blank lines between each new thought, and be sure to write down rather than across the card as it makes it easier to find your place.
- Do not write an entire sentence, just a few words to help you bring the thought to mind.
- No matter how familiar you are with names and titles, print them on the cards; those are among the easiest things to forget.
- Number each of the cards in the upper right-hand corner. This is especially important because a cue card out of place can throw you off balance quite easily.
- Before you leave home and close your door behind you, check and double check that you have them — *all* of them — with you. At home on the piano, they are of no help.

Should you have such a traumatic lapse of memory that, even with the cue cards, you forget your place (and this certainly is not apt to happen), give yourself a minute — ask someone in the audience to recap your last point for you, and go on. If you do not make it a paramount issue, it will be forgotten before your speech is over.

Sometimes you can wage a battle with yourself over the uselessness of allowing nerves to attack out of control, and after assaulting them with all the facts, may still feel a little shaky. You must stage an aggressive, all-out war, and be as persistent as they are to win. Here is an additional wave or reinforcement to smash through their stubborn surges of tension. You can defeat them if you employ these positive approaches.

- Realize fully why you have been asked to speak. It must be because you know more about the subject, have had more experience, or are more involved than anyone else there. If someone else could speak with more authority, the chairman would have invited her to address the group. You most certainly will never be asked to give a talk on something you know nothing about. Since you are sharing your expertise, you have every right to feel comfortable and enthusiastic. Take the reins and tell yourself that you are in command, and show it.

- Adopt the motto of the Holiday Inn Motels that "No surprise is the best surprise," and plan ahead to have it that way. Send your introducer on to the liaison person. Know ahead if you are to use a mike, how many other speakers there will be on the program, and if you will be on a stage, behind a head table or at a rostrum on the floor level. Walk into a familiar setting.

- If you are using any visual aids, be sure to check the suggestions for encompassing them in the chapter on "Tips For The Career Woman — The Business Talk."

- Plan ahead what you will wear. A long gown, business suit or short dress will depend upon the program and if you are not sure about the formality of the affair, check on it well in advance. Whatever the mode of dress, keep it simple. Sleeveless dresses should not be worn without a jacket. No dangling earrings or bracelets — no diamonds or jewelry that will catch the lights and outsparkle you — nothing that is ostentatious, as it interrupts the attention that should be directed solely to your message. Never wear new, slippery shoes, and, above all, don't switch heel heights. Basic, flattering and comfortable are your key words.

- Give yourself more than ample time to arrive, allowing for traffic hold-ups and any other possible delay.
- Be thoroughly prepared. Never just think a talk through — say it out loud, many times, using the volume you feel you will employ when on stage. If you do not practice out loud, your own voice will fool you and possibly confuse you.
- Take your time. Once you have been introduced, it is your meeting. Take that deep breath, thank the person who introduced you, and smile. Greet your audience and relax your body.
- If you wear glasses only for reading, do not put them on until you need them. If you have both dark and clear prescription glasses, it is preferable to wear the clear ones to keep the most direct contact with your audience.
- Stand tall. Posture is of prime importance. Relax your shoulders, but never slump. Everything about you must say, "I know my subject and I enjoy sharing it with you." Your bearing is a mirror reflection of your mental attitude and it will telegraph insecurities and nervousness.
- Gesture at any time that it feels comfortable, but never fidget. Tapping of fingers, playing with jewelry, shuffling cue cards or any other nervous habit must be eliminated, or it will command more attention than you receive.
- Look at your audience. You will find them friendly and supportive. It will enable you to establish a rapport, so that you are talking with them and not above them.

If there is one mortal sin to be avoided at all times by a new speaker, it is this. Never — NEVER talk with anyone about how nervous you feel. Never even allow yourself to think about it, even for a short period of time. If you indulge in telling someone else that you don't know how you'll get through it, you are so tense you can't swallow, you don't know what you'll do if you forget (of course, you know what you'll do — you just read all about it), you just know your hands will shake, etc., etc., you will put yourself into such a state that it will be impossible for you to do well. Even thinking such thoughts is a speaker's occasion of sin. When you realize that you are growing tense, stop, take a deep breath and force positive thoughts into your mind. You look great — it's a friendly group — you are well prepared — they will be most receptive — you are bursting with enthusiasm. (You simply misinterpreted the feeling — it is enthusiasm!)

After conducting a highly successful meeting, the chairman was complimented on her poise and pleasant self-assurance. "I can't believe," she said, "that I am the same woman who shook and started to cry when I had to make an announcement to the Brownie mothers."

You can do it, too. It is only a two step procedure. Think about it — Act upon it.

## Prepare Yourself

Now that you have made up your mind to speak as soon as an occasion arises, it is time to start to prepare and rehearse. (Be sure that you do not confuse "preparing" with "worrying." They are not synonymous and the latter is completely useless.) Standing and facing a group is the initial step, and for many the most difficult. Practice at every opportunity. If you are asking or answering a question in your adult education class, stand to do it. If you are to read a report at a meeting, stand and walk to the front of the room. (Never again ask, "Is it all right if I just read it from here?") At the end of your coffee break, stand when you say, "Shall we return to our desks?" At the town meeting, stand up and ask the councilman to speak up so that those of you in the back of the hall can hear more easily. Each time you speak out, remind yourself that once again you have successfully addressed a group. It is a simple matter to do it for a little longer period of time. When the day arrives that you are asked (or, that you volunteer) to be a main speaker, you know you are experienced, at least, in standing and speaking up.

Now, be that same person when the speech situation becomes a bit more formal. You will be your best when you are *yourself, at your best*. Although you have studied others and found how they are most dynamic, you should adopt only their mechanics, and never their personality. The speaker you most wish to emulate may tell a joke well, but if it is not your style, it will not do well for you. Nothing is as unnerving as looking for a laugh that doesn't come. Concentrate on her other techniques and adopt them to your manner of presentation.

Before your first word has been spoken, your posture and your facial expression will have made an impression on your audience. From the moment you are introduced, you are in charge — every facet of your physical and mental being must convey that fact. You need not be drill sergeant military, but you do need to stand straight, on both feet, and both hips (no one-hip slouch will do), with your head up and a firm step. Your facial expression should say, "Hello, I'm pleased to be here," before your voice has a chance to announce it. Look directly at your audience when you smile and greet them, and throughout your talk. When you look from one side of the group to the other, turn your head and never just your eyes. Include everyone. Your gestures should be full to reinforce what you are saying. Quick, jerky gestures tend to confuse and give you the appearance of one who is unsure and nervous. Your arms should be relaxed and not held rigidly against your sides.

If you are seated, your posture is equally important. Do not lean back into the chair or your body language will telegraph a ho-hum attitude. When serving on a panel, it is well to take note of the fact that the table is not usually covered by a cloth, and it requires that you take special care that you look as well composed and dignified below your waist as you do above it. Knees together, skirts down, and if you wish to cross your legs, it should be at the ankle, rather than at the knees.

If you are using cue cards for any reason while taking part in a panel seated on stage, try to refer to them only occasionally, and then while someone else is speaking. If you are the only speaker, and standing at a podium, place the cue cards as high as possible. It will be easier for you to find your place and it will be possible for you to check them easily without your head and eyes noticeably bouncing up and down. If you wear glasses to read, put them on at the start of your talk and leave them on until you are finished. Should you have both glasses and contacts available, contacts are a better choice, as they do not catch the lights as glasses are prone to do, and they are one less thing for you to handle.

Whenever you practice, and it should be often, always verbalize your speech. That is the time to catch words or phrases which are apt to give you trouble and if your transitions do not sound smooth, you can rethink them. If you have a tape recorder, turn it on each time you go over your speech and play it back several times to be sure you hear all the parts repeatedly and can make every necessary correction. If your voice sounds a little high to you, place your cue cards on the floor, sit in a hard chair, let your upper body lean forward and go over your talk again, facing the floor. You will hear your voice come down to the lower pitch for which you are striving.

## How To Emphasize Your Points

For those very important parts of your speech that you want the audience to remember above all others, you must employ some verbal punctuation. There are several ways to do this. You may change position, perhaps coming closer to your audience by walking to the side of the podium (if you are not using a mike) or by changing the tempo of your speech, either speaking more quickly and urgently, or more slowly and deliberately. You may repeat a word or phrase. The least effective method is to yell! Yelling only emphasizes once — and loses its effectiveness quickly.

Within public speaking circles, there is a favorite and often told story about a minister who was renown for his dramatic and forceful sermons. One Sunday he left his notes on the pulpit and the next morning the caretaker found them there. He noticed that each place that the minister wanted to emphasize, he had marked an appropriate means of doing so in the margin. At one point, a notation said, "Lift arms to heaven here," and another, "Pound fist here." On the third card, underlined, were the words — "Weakest argument, yell like h---!"

The strongest form of emphasis you can employ is the pause. It forces the listener's mind to speak with you. You will notice that in most T.V. and radio commercials, a seasoned announcer will always pause for a moment before giving the name of a product he wants you to remember. Late in the evening, when a familiar voice from Hollywood says, "And here'ssssssss ----------," millions of mental voices add "Johnnie" before he does. It is perhaps the most famous introduction in the nation, next to, "Ladies and gentlemen," PAUSE, "the President of the United States."

While giving thought to the presentation of the body of the speech, don't forget to make plans for the question period. You are still on stage and you don't want to lose the favorable impression you have created by neglecting the final few minutes. T.S. Eliot's famous line, in the "Hollow Men," predicted that the world would end "not with a bang, but with a whimper." This must never apply to the conclusion of your speech. The cymbals must clash to cue the applause. Because this is so important, there is a full chapter entitled, "The Question Period," to help you successfully conclude your presentation.

Some speakers are asked to repeat the same speech many times, just as musicians play the same music again and again. Never allow a repeat performance to lull you into complacency. Each audience is a new audience. (Teachers and tour guides take special note.) Each has a right to hear the same vital material as the group that preceded it. Plays run for years on Broadway, but professionals make them come alive with every performance. Review, critique and improve each time you offer your talk. The "I've done this so many times, now I don't even have to think about it" school of thought has never yet graduated a professional. If you are an "after dinner," "after luncheon," or "just before coffee break" speaker, you still want what you say to be remembered and talked about more than the food that was served.

What about your menu? Don't make the mistake of thinking that because you are a little tense, you cannot eat. It may be better not to have a heavy meal, and never a dozen cups of coffee, but unless you want your stomach to make more sounds than you behind the mike, you had best partake of something light. It is easier to munch on soup and crackers than to stop a growling stomach or hiccups once they've started. You should, however, avoid milk and beer before you speak, as both form mucous, and you may find yourself clearing your throat repeatedly. Needless to say, the time for a cocktail is after your talk, for congratulations, and never, never ahead of time for false courage. Librium, or any other form of medication used to relax, will only lull you into being less than your best. You need that touch of anxiety to whip up into all the enthusiasm you want to share with your listeners. When you have left the platform, that is the time to completely relax, and you will not need a pill to do it then. Be sure you maintain your control right through the time you leave, and never be caught sighing, looking to heaven or sticking your tongue out in relief when your audience starts to applaud.

Practice being confident. Self-confidence, just like happiness, is a state of mind. Both are such nice things to have, you should make a gift of them to yourself, and keep them for a lifetime.

## Preparing Your Speech

Author's Note: The purpose of this chapter is not to dissect the mechanics of the various types of speeches. The toastmaster's speech, highly technical speeches and political speeches are not covered. We will deal here only with the general, short, informative talk that you will be most likely to give. We will cover the basics of a talk from five to twenty minutes, and when you feel comfortable and can speak effectively for that length of time, you will have no difficulty in finding additional material in your library that will help you to move on, if you wish to do so.

## The Beginning

The most difficult part of composing most speeches, for the majority of people, is finding a way to begin. It can be made easy by coming to grips with two basic questions. "What is my purpose — to inform, entertain, report, pay tribute or introduce someone else?" The next thing that must be clear in your mind is, "How long do I intend to speak?" You may think you will have trouble filling three minutes, but once into your subject find that, thirty minutes later, you still have points you wish to include. Timing is important, and when in doubt, shorten.

## Choosing Your Subject

Within the framework of your purpose, you may be able to choose from among several subjects. Give careful thought to what it will be, for on this one answer rests your entire speech. Don't attempt ever — under any circumstances — to speak on something with which you are not personally familiar, no matter how intriguing the idea may be. The research you do on your program should be only to check facts or expand some areas, but it should never have to be on the fundamental concepts. There may be times when you are asked to discuss something as familiar as your own work, but if it is not comfortable for you, change the approach and thrust of the subject until you find the appeal you want. For example: the fashionable owner of an elite, modern bridal shop was asked to address a group of high school girls on the best methods of selecting bridal gowns. Although she was superbly qualified, she felt that the focus of her talk was not correct for girls still so young. She solved her problem by approaching the subject from the viewpoint of selecting a bridesmaid's gown, and their duties and responsibilities in that role, and how, in addition, they could be helpful to an older sister who was shopping for a bridal gown. Now she believed in her subject and her talk was highly successful.

Should the subject you decide upon have many facets, select only one. In speaking to your music club on your recent tour of the Orient, cover only one adventure and then pare away the details. They might be interested in hearing about the Festival of Folk Music you attended in China — but not what time you boarded the plane — the delays, etc., etc. You may also be expected to answer questions and the broader your topic, the wider range of questions you will be asked. No one can be expected to have the answers to all questions at her instant command, but she should know at least the ones pertinent to her subject. That is why politicians select issues and wisely refuse to discuss any topics which deviate from them or on which they may not be fully briefed.

## An Opening Sentence

Now you are comfortable and enthused about your topic and your next step is to immediately whet the interest of your audience. Your opening sentence and your closing sentence are the two most important statements, interest-wise, that you will make, and the only exceptions to the rule that nothing should be memorized, word for word. You must make your audience sit up and rivet their attention on you. Never start by saying, "The title of the subject I am going to speak on tonight is . . ." That is a certain death penalty introduction to any speech. This is your chance to be innovative, to use your imagination and show a flair for the dramatic. Here are some examples that brought members of various speech classes to attention.

"Ten thousand people committed suicide last year with guns — but today, over one hundred thousand took steps to do the same thing by using this death weapon." She then held up a packet of granulated sugar and went on to talk about the health food store she was opening with her husband.

Another woman looked at the class, paused for a moment (very effective) and then said, "There is no point in my trying to deny it, all our friends know now that my husband and I spend our weekends bending our elbows." Another pause while a surprised class reacted. They then were told how the couple collected and re-sold antique glass, after carefully checking the imprints on the bottom of each piece.

One young girl seemed to be off on the wrong foot, but she wasn't. "I hope you are all comfortable," she said, "because I have 32 different topics to talk about tonight," then slowly, "your teeth."

A middle-aged woman shook her head solemnly as she announced, "I have made a most unexpected discovery in this class. I have found a classmate who, all of her adult life, has been in love with the same man that I love. We both live near his home and have spent time there, and yet we never knew about each other." She confessed to all her listeners of a long love affair shared with her new friend, for Norman Rockwell and his paintings.

There are as many attention gaining ways to start as there are topics, and a little thought will embark you on your subject with full audience curiosity. Other than catching the immediate interest of the audience, is there any other way to begin? No.

So many professional speakers bring about this attention with humor, that often the amateur feels it is the best of all possible beginnings. It is worth repeating that only those who are completely at ease and have sure fire material (sure fire for them, not Bob Newhart), should incorporate a joke as an introduction. A warm smile that encompasses the entire group, will bring a friendly smile in response, and is more welcome and far more effective than a poorly told story.

## The Body Of The Speech

You know your purpose, you have decided how to arouse audience interest, and what you will say to command their complete attention. Now is the time to communicate. The word itself comes from the Latin, "communicatus" which means "to share," and that is the key to all that you plan now.

A simple outline is the easiest way to start. Your major headings will be:
- My purpose
- Information to be included
- Facts that back my statements
- Action I want the audience to take
- Strong ending

Now, write down the major points to be covered. They don't have to be in the order in which you will finally present them. The important thing is to collect them so you can evaluate and eliminate. Write down every thought that comes to you. When you have them on paper, you can cut each one off and rearrange them, jigsaw-puzzle fashion, until the exact picture you are to present is emerging. If you have trouble, start by writing the simple sentence, "What I want to tell you is . . ." Later, you will discard that for the more creative introduction you have already written. Check, now, that what you are going to tell the audience relates to them. You must know your material and your audience.

Richard C. Garvey, editor of the Springfield Daily News, presented an excellent example of relating to an audience when he welcomed the Travel Writers' Convention to the City of Springfield for the Chamber of Commerce. Mr. Garvey took the time to research the area represented by each group of writers and then told of a direct connection between their area and the history of the City of Springfield. Not only did it prove to be a fascinating historical speech, but it also gave a warm and strikingly personal welcome to the visitors. They will remember Mr. Garvey's city and feel a kinship with it long after other events have been forgotten.

Once you have your facts on paper, check them out to reaffirm their accuracy (the same should be done with quotes). One incorrect piece of information will make your entire speech suspect. If you forcefully announce that the Child's Garden of Verse was written by Longfellow, instead of Stevenson, the audience may later have their doubts if you tell them Romeo and Juliet is the work of Shakespeare.

When you have your information and your background facts in order, express them in your own way. You may have heard someone else give a brilliant talk on your subject, but that was her talk, and it was effective because it was uniquely her own. You want to instill your personality into what you are saying, so say it with the vocabulary that comes naturally to you, and not with words you feel sound more impressive. If a phrase or sentence feels uncomfortable, reword it. It probably needs to be simplified. Perhaps a point would be better told in another form if it were to be written in an article, but you are preparing a talk.

There is a distinct difference between the effective spoken word and a strongly written sentence. The spoken word should be kept simple and more direct. You may have at sometime been disappointed when you found that an excellent author was not a commanding speaker. The written word is much more tolerant of long descriptions and detailed word picture drawings. "She was a vision of efficiency and mercy as she hurried from wounded soldier to wounded soldier, never for a moment mindful of the danger exploding around her," might be acceptable in some war stories, but behind a rostrum it would never snap an audience to attention. An entire chapter of terse, short, clipped sentences might bore a reader, while proving electrifying when fired in rapid succession by a powerful speaker. You must make your own punctuation when you speak. The periods, exclamation points and question marks are all in your voice, and you must use them. A bit more liberty can be taken with grammar, at times, to gain the desired results. It is said that Sir Winston Churchill, often quoted for his sparkling wit, submitted a speech he had written to his proofreader for major corrections. When it was returned to him a sentence that he had written was questioned. He looked at his wording, which said, "We must ask who they are working for," and saw it underlined in red, and a notation in the margin which read, "You have ended this sentence with a preposition." Churchill promptly underlined the correction in red, and returned it, with the notation, "This is the kind of nonsense, up with which, I will not put!" The speaker has only one chance to effect action, and every word must be dynamic.

It is wise to avoid long lists and large doses of statistics. If you use some statistics or percentage figures, make them relevant. "That is twice the number of people that you saw attending the Super Bowl game." Draw a mental picture that can be easily comprehended.

Present only the most pertinent facts. No matter how impressive or well documented your points may be, there is always a line between all the audience wants to know and more than it cares to know. When in doubt, cut. Even fascinating material can be dulled by length. A talk on "The Sinking of the Lusitania" can be awesome, but hearing "A chronological description of all German and American ships sunk in the two major wars" is too much for most to comprehend.

Whatever the end you wish to achieve, whatever response you are working for, you will obtain it most successfully if you make your message relate directly to every person there. If you were asked to recruit women to help with the local Girl Scout troops, which of the following approaches do you think would gain the greatest results?

"The Girl Scouts are truly a worthwhile organization and they are in need of help. They are a national organization and stress good citizenship in their members. It doesn't take much time and anyone who is interested can find out more about them by visiting their headquarters on Main Street. Their telephone number is in the phone book and you can call any day. They will appreciate any help you can give them. If you don't have the time, perhaps you could tell a friend or neighbor about the Girl Scouts. They will enjoy working with the girls and other leaders." — or —

"Betty Sue is now eight years old. She is slightly handicapped and she needs your help. She wants to become a Girl Scout, but there is not a single volunteer to give three hours a week to open a troop for Betty Sue and her five friends. If you are qualified, there is no pay — no glory — no publicity, but there is the respect and friendship of six little girls, and we hope that is of greater value. I'll be happy to work with you, answer your questions and put you in touch with the chapter that desperately needs you now."

Both are exactly the same number of words.

One additional suggestion. It can be quite forceful in a speech to repeat the same word or phrase for effect, as long as it is not a cliche. Others may espouse their concern with "burning issues," and "feedback," at "this point in time," but don't you be guilty of that deathly dullness!

## The End

When you have fulfilled your purpose — end. It should be well within the time frame you set for yourself at the beginning. You should not announce that you are ending, nor threaten, nor warn; you should simply end positively, forcefully or dramatically. Never simply run down. Your voice, your words and your enthusiasm should build right to the end. Your last sentence, as your first, may be memorized, but along with the rest of your speech, it should be subject to change as your audience changes. If you have been speaking to your co-workers about new merchandising techniques adopted in your department, you will present it in a different format than when you discuss the same subject with the local Business and Professional Women's Club. Know your subject well enough to be flexible when presenting it.

Ask for and graciously receive suggestions and criticisms on your talk. Weigh them objectively, incorporate those you feel have merit, and discard those that are not pertinent, or petty.

If you are not completely satisfied with the response you received, perhaps you can solve your problem by checking it against the following list of questions.

1. Was it appropriate?
2. Did it have a clear point?
3. Did I outline and organize it?
4. Was I enthused about it?
5. Did I try to communicate that enthusiasm?

6. Was I confident and relaxed about my appearance?
7. Did I walk and stand with a positive attitude?
8. Did I make eye contact?
9. Did I speak directly to my audience?
10. Did my voice reinforce my message?
11. Did I articulate well, so that I was easily understood?
12. Was I pleasant, displaying an empathy with my audience?

Perhaps, there should be one more question. Am I being unreasonably critical of myself?

# Chapter Thirteen

## The Question Period

Unless the Speech you are to give comes under the heading of Testimonial or Sermon, you may safely anticipate questions. Indeed, if there are no questions you may not have been a very dynamic speaker. It would then be wise for you to reassess your talk and its presentation. Ask the program chairman when you are making arrangements if she would like to have you entertain questions, and the time limit she would like set on that period. Be sure to review this information with the person who will introduce you so that she may include it in her material. Should she forget to do so, mention it yourself sometime near the beginning of your talk. Perhaps between the introduction and the body of your talk would be an easy place to insert it without throwing you off beat.

What Happens If No One Asks Me The First Question?

In the majority of cases hands will start waving before the last of the applause dies down, and there is no problem to consider. However, you will find the pace will vary a bit depending on the amount of self-consciousness there is among those in your audience. Women who have purchased tickets to a seminar being held in a department store, and largely strangers to one another, are a bit more reluctant to be the first to speak out than are the women attending a club meeting where they are familiar and comfortable speaking before old friends. It is only the first question which may bring a hesitation. Once that has been asked the others will flow right along.

There are several ways you can help your audience over that initial hurdle. Some speakers plant a question with a friend to start things going. This has the additional benefit of giving the speaker a chance to extend her platform on a subject she may wish to expand, or return attention to a specific area of her talk. People with causes and politicians are reputed to often seed their audiences in this manner.

If planting questions isn't your style, there are other effective starters. Do not make the mistake of asking, "Aren't there any questions? Doesn't anyone have a question to ask?" It is a negative approach, and you are making each person more self-conscious about asking the first one. Instead try asking the question yourself.

"I am often asked if I feel . . ." or "At a meeting in Boston I found many of the suburban women wanted to know . . ."

This way you have taken them over the hurdle of the first question, and psychologically the next person to speak is asking the second question. It is extremely unlikely that you would ever need to present more than one question. You might, for dire emergencies, have two ready. And if there was still no response, you'd simply have to write it off, thank them and leave graciously.

If your subject is highly controversial and you know people might feel awkward asking questions, or if you have been forewarned that this particular audience is always reluctant to address the speaker, make arrangements ahead of time for written questions to be submitted to you. This will lead to a verbal exchange within a very short time.

A far more typical situation is an abundance of questions. If you have held the interest of your audience and injected your enthusiasm into them, they will be anxious to join in. You can expect a wide variety of questions and you should be as prepared for this portion of your program as you were for your presentation. You are still on center stage. Let's consider the most professional way to hold and control the question period now that you have it started and it's moving into full swing.

- Always start by repeating the question. This insures that you have heard it correctly and that the entire audience knows what is being discussed. It also stops the confusion that comes from people asking each other what was asked. Address the entire audience when you answer.
- Try to keep your answers relatively short. If you give an additional speech with each answer people will hesitate to ask questions.
- Always be patient. If you explained the point three times within your talk, reword it briefly again. Never belittle or embarrass, and above all, never laugh at a question sincerely asked.
- Be sure you can back up statistics and quotes without fumbling through cue cards. It is a good idea to have this information on a separate card written for the question period, and at your fingertips in case it is asked for and your memory fails you.
- If the question is an intricate one, or one that is only of concern to the person presenting it, you should indicate that you will be happy to review it in detail with her and suggest that she meet with you directly at the close of the session.

> Example: After a talk on speaking in public with confidence, a woman might ask, "My daughter has a tendency to lisp, and

she is quite self-conscious about it. I wonder if you could tell me if there is any way I can help her at home, or how I can go about finding a qualified speech therapist?"

"Yes, I'd be happy to give you some suggestions. If you have a minute I'd be glad to go over them with you right after the program. Please come up and see me then."

Since this is not the subject you are addressing, it requires that you answer it at another time.
- When a question is too long, try to reword it concisely when you repeat it to the audience so that it is more easily understood.
- If the question is completely irrelevant, simply respond that it is an excellent question — or a thought-provoking question — but perhaps best considered at another time, as it is essential within your time frame to restrict the discussion to your topic.
- Never allow the platform to be taken away from you. Occasionally, you will find someone with a speech of her own, ready to be delivered on your time. Be polite but firm and never intimidate. Interrupt if you must and ask to go over her ideas with her later.
- Limit within reason one person to one question. How often have you heard a dialogue develop between a speaker and one member of the audience, while others grew impatient waiting for their turn.
- Never be afraid to say, "I don't know," Never bluff. Even if it is a question you should have the answer to, be honest. (Bet no one will ever catch

you on that one again!) Admit you will have to check on it — tell them where the information would be available if you know, or if it is important, offer to mail it to them and then be sure you do. (There are many definitions of a well-educated person; one that is especially helpful says, "A well-educated person does not know everything — but does know where to find it.")
- Never end the question period after an "I don't know" answer. Both your Speech and your question period should end positively.
- Be willing to stand corrected. Thank the person if she has politely pointed out an error and you have reason to feel she is correct. You are expected to be knowledgeable but not necessarily infallible. (This is not an excuse for being careless or sloppy in your research, and it should always be the exceptional circumstance.)
- Don't be defensive. If you are confident of your facts and position, don't be upset if your ideas or methods are questioned, or another view expressed. You are offering what you have found to be right, and has worked best and proven reliable for you. Thank the person for presenting another view, state that you are always interested, but don't dissolve or feel it is necessary to march into battle.

    Example: "You said the speaker should always look at her audience and establish eye contact, but I took a correspondence course in public speaking, and I was definitely told it was better to look over the tops of everyone's heads and then you wouldn't be so nervous." (Notice that is a statement, not a question, so there is no need to explain your reasons, as they haven't been asked.)

"That is completely different from my approach, but it is interesting and I thank you for sharing it."

- Be prepared for personal questions to suddenly pop up. They are most often asked in sincere interest and should be handled tactfully. Snappy, curt answers may be fun to read, but usually unnecessary to give. If you make one person feel uncomfortable you'll make your entire audience uneasy. If the question was in poor taste, everyone is aware of it, and you'll be more admired for your tact than for your biting wit in your answer.
- Know when to bring the period to a close. Only when you are in a teaching situation should you continue on until all questions are answered. For any other audience it is best to end while interest is still high. There is no more boring ending than, "Are there any more questions? Are you sure there isn't anything else you want to ask me? Did we cover everything? Well then, if you're sure you haven't any more questions, I guess that's all." Everyone sincerely hopes so! Let's go!

# Chapter Fourteen

## Why You Should Study Public Speaking If You Are Never Going To Speak In Public

> Nothing in life is to be
> feared, only understood.
> — Marie Curie

There is, of course, no such thing as going from the cradle to the grave without ever speaking in public. Your audiences may not number in the thousands, but you have an audience. The average person speaks over 5,000 words a day, and that's a great deal of talking to have done in private! Every day, as soon as you speak to someone, your voice makes an impression. Your audience of one, or three or seven, decides right at that point if you are cheerful, tired, upset, impatient or optimistic. They decide if they would enjoy more of your company, or would just as soon you were on your way. You may never want to use your voice to recruit your fellow citizens to cast their vote in your behalf, but if you'd like the sales clerk to check something in the stockroom for you, you stand a better chance if your voice is pleasing to her.

It is not just for you that we say a speech course is important. It is for those speeches to which we listen. Daily you form the core of your convictions by listening to what other people are telling you. On the radio, on the TV, from the pulpit and in the public forum — you are told what others would like you to think, what they want you to join, how they expect your support and how they demand you cast your ballot. Usually, they are polished, effective speakers. They know exactly what they are doing — and so should you.

Supposing someone wants you to accept a proposition she is not entirely sure you're going to buy. In the back of your mind, you have an idea what she is going to say, and you're skeptical about it. You're sitting there with a "well, let's hear what you've got to say" attitude. Then the speaker walks up to the mike, smiles and tells you a funny story. Usually a ridiculous or embarrassing thing where she is the butt of the joke. Pretty soon you are laughing with her. Did you ever try to argue with someone who has you laughing? It's a pretty difficult thing to do. Twenty minutes later you're saying, "She really is a pretty down-to-earth person. I thought she was great and what she said made a lot of sense, too." Did it? Let's hope so.

How about the speaker who wants to convince you of her point of view? She may start on common ground. Something in the line of a question that will get a sure 'yes'. "I'm sure we all love our country?" She enlarges upon it — "We are proud to be Americans," etc. Heads all over the hall nod 'yes'. A second statement, "We work hard for what we have. Our fathers fought for freedom, our brothers and sisters fought for it, and our sons and daughters fought. Many of you sitting here tonight fought." Watch all the heads nodding and affirming. The third statement, "We don't want to see anyone hungry in our country," etc., etc. More 'yes, true, yes' nods. Whatever she says next will get a fourth 'yes' by a large majority of the audience. No one knows exactly why three 'yes' answers equal four 'yes' answers, but any teacher of Platform Art will confirm that it works. Even the boy at your door selling anything has his sale almost assured if he can first get you to agree that 1) it's a nice day, 2) you live on a well-kept street, and 3) your dog is the greatest.

How about the way questions are answered? Do you always hear an answer?

If the politician says: "I'm glad you asked that — it gives me a chance to tell you . . ." I'll bet if you were really listening you didn't hear the question that you asked, answered.

If you mention that you understand from TV reports that the Starvation Awareness program the speaker has just praised has not given one cent of its money to relieve starvation, and you'd like to know if this is true, and the speaker says —

"That's an interesting comment — I didn't happen to see that program, but even more pertinent etc., etc." or "First let me tell you . . ."

Where's your answer?

How about people who use endorsements to persuade? "The Vet's of Foreign Wars are behind me 100% — to a man. How about you?" He may be exaggerating a bit.

Or association — "The party of Washington, Jefferson, Lincoln and me!"

Do you know what you are listening to, and why you are forming opinions? You should.

Is this manner of presentation wrong? No, absolutely not! If you have a good product, or a worthwhile cause, why shouldn't you offer it in the most attractive way possible? You should. If you believe in something and want support it would be foolish not to seek it out as effectively as possible, wouldn't it? Because something is well-packaged doesn't mean it is defective. What the speaker is saying may be exactly right and deserving of complete co-operation. It is simply prudent of you to know exactly why you enrolled in a cause. It is the duty of every person today to immunize herself against manipulation, and to do this you must be able to distinguish the gift from the wrapping. Fancy boxes are fun, but they don't always indicate the value of the article inside. Know what you are buying and why. If you sit in a good Public Speaking class and never say a word, but you learn how to listen, you have become a far wiser person.

When Adolf Hitler spoke, he was one of the most dynamic, enthused and forceful speakers of his time. A man who listened to him in person once said he could not disagree with Hitler while he was speaking. Only after he went home and reviewed the talk in his mind, step by step, could he see the diabolical fallacies in Hitler's plans. Nothing, absolutely nothing, is more powerful for good or evil than the human voice. Understand it — it is your privilege and your duty.

# Chapter Fifteen

## Let's Look At How You Listen

Why?

You are reading about Speech. You are working on methods to enhance your voice, your diction, your articulation and your credibility — how does this chapter on listening suddenly emerge? It seems so simple, when you are not speaking, you are listening. Sometimes you are paying attention, and sometimes you are not. It is the question of how attentively you listen that will be considered now, because it is almost equal in importance to how effectively you speak. Listening plays a major role in every aspect of your social and professional life.

Can You Identify the Caring People in a Public Place?

Have you ever had an occasion to dine in a public dining room by yourself? It's a great opportunity to do some people watching.

For starters, a casual glance around the room will tell you quite accurately which women, at the tables for two, are caring and interacting with their dinner partners. If a woman is focusing her attention on the person she is with, if she is contributing to but not monopolizing the conversation and listens with undivided attention, she is projecting a sincere interest. Chief among the above clues is the way she listens — completely absorbed in what he says. (Reversing this test proves to be just as accurate. How attentive is her partner to her conversation?)

Some years ago a woman found herself having dinner in the same hotel as the Duke and Duchess of Windsor. She was seated only a table from them and she remembers that every diner there was acutely aware of the presence of the famous couple, but that they seemed oblivious to all the eyes that were on them. The Duchess gave full attention to her husband. She never once glanced away from their table and between courses (manners not withstanding), she placed both elbows on the table, put her chin in her hands, and looked so captivated by his conversation that it appeared she could not hear enough of what this delightful, charming man had to tell her. Although they had been married for many years by that time, the Duchess still complimented him by offering her undivided attention. When she spoke, her eyes still focused only on the Duke and she appeared vital and enthusiastic.

By the dozens, magazine articles will tell you to be a good listener, but most don't tell you the exact steps to take to develop this asset. Some will advise that many women are thought to be superlative conversationalists, merely because they pay attention and allow others to do the talking. That is not an accurate statement. Being a good listener does not mean being a non-contributor. Is there anything more frustrating than trying to inch a conversation from someone who only ah's and uh-huh's you, and answers every question with a monosyllable? You work so hard and gain so little that you soon decide the effort isn't worth it and move on to someone who is more than just barely alive and breathing.

Newstand periodicals often suggest that to prove that you are a "sincere and vitally concerned human being" you need only to show an interest in the other person. This is done by erasing yourself from the conversation and asking questions about the other person's work, interests, family and views. While a general question or two may be an excellent starter, its use should be limited. If your conversation is simply a long list of questions without any additional input on your part, you don't have a conversation — you have an inquisition. Far from being flattered, the person you have just met is more apt to feel put upon, smothered and anxious to escape. There is more to listening than keeping still, and more to becoming a caring person than issuing a third degree. Try taking a look at the subject and see if you can find areas in which you may be able to improve your listening skills.

### How Do You Rate Your Listening Ability?

First, see how you score yourself on a Good Listener's Test. If you have already developed excellent habits, you may wish to skip the remainder of this chapter and move right along to the next one, with a big plus mark in your column. Don't answer the questions too quickly. It is easy to confuse what you know is right with that which you actually do. This test has been compiled from a great number of text book questionnaires on the subject by women in various speech classes who rated the tests as they applied to their lives. Here are the twelve questions they felt were the most important.

1. Do you enjoy listening, or would you usually prefer to do the talking?
2. Is it easy for you to listen with interest to a large variety of subjects, or do you find yourself wishing the conversation would revert back to a speech area of concern to you?
3. Do your friends seek you out to discuss a problem or decision when they need help?
4. Does your attention usually stray toward other groups, or people entering or leaving the room?
5. Do you interrupt?

6. Are you more apt to be thinking ahead to what you will say next than weighing what you are being told?
7. Be honest now — Do you stop listening to everything when you strongly disagree with the speaker on one point?
8. Do you assume or anticipate regarding the other person's views?
9. Do you feel you can judge most people quite quickly, before hearing them out?
10. Do you generalize? (All these old people think; all college kids are radicals; all government employees are lazy.)
11. Do you encourage others to elaborate or clarify points you may have misunderstood?
12. Do you listen to what is not said? (The tone of voice — the obvious omission.)

Review in your mind a recent conversation and see if you can remember most of the details. If you catch yourself saying, "I don't remember exactly what she said about her trip," or "I think she said they tried a certain procedure, but I can't think what the results were," you may not have been paying attention.

There is another habit that goes hand in hand with lack of concentration and is often undetected. Do you: ask the person with whom you are talking if she will repeat something again that you heard the first time? It is often a play for time, or it may be just unintentional carelessness. It should never be allowed to become a habit.

It is easy to justify poor listening habits. Every day there are hours of unnecessary talk. For most people a fantasy of peace and solitude includes nothing more harsh on the eardrums than wind, waves and seagulls.

It is easy to learn how to "tune out" the frivolous

banter, but that is a luxury which must be restricted. It has no place in personal relationships. You must not only listen, you must also hear what is being said. That may be quite different from what you want to hear and often only that which pleases us is heard, regardless of what is spoken.

There is no question that if you are to advance in business, concentrated listening is an absolute requirement (see chapter on "Tips for the Career Woman") and if you want to improve your relationships with others, it will pay enormous dividends. Here are the hallmarks of a good listener.

— This above all — she gives her complete attention. She never allows her interest to be interrupted. This is most easily accomplished by keeping eye contact.

— She encourages others to talk freely by refraining from interrupting and never topping what they have to say. While not questioning endlessly, an occasional question, or simply a nod of the head, an "I understand," or "Of course" is sufficient.

— Being selective and never allowing herself to be imposed upon with pettiness or nonsense (her time is of value) she makes judgment and is patient if circumstances warrant it.

— She only listens and makes no moral judgment unless she is asked for an opinion. (The exception, of course, is in giving sound guidance to your children or those for whom you are responsible.)

— She never leads people, by questions or encouragement, to relate more than they wish to say.

— She never joins in criticism of another woman's husband, children, co-workers or relatives, and certainly never expands on them. Families fortunately patch matters up, but what is said by others is not easily forgotten.

— She has established a reputation that makes a speaker secure in her integrity, knowing that she will never betray a confidence or bring up a subject again, once it has been settled.

— She is sensitive to the feelings of others and makes an earnest effort to see their point of view and establish an empathy with them. If their convictions are completely opposite to her personal standards, she never deserts her principles — apologizes for them — or ignores them. She is always tactfully honest.

— She doesn't downplay her own stature. (Usually, people prefer to discuss matters with those they feel have good judgment, intelligence and convictions.)

## What Are You Listening To?

Be as careful about what your mind digests as you are about the food you eat. Give serious thought to what is said, and how it is presented. (Be sure to read the chapter on "Why You Should Study Public Speaking If You Are Never Going To Speak In Public." It will point out to you some of the more common ways people can use to convince you of ideas that do not merit your approval, and you should be aware of them and be watchful.) Weigh objectively a rousing talk on any subject before you enlist and carry a banner. Remember, in most situations you are hearing only one person's view. Think, and then draw a conclusion. Once you have a carefully thought out stand, unless there is new, overwhelming evidence, stand by it. Establishing a firm set of lasting values is a sure sign of both maturity and confidence. There are rare times when a change is in order, but blowing in a different direction with each big wind doesn't prove an open mind — only holes in the head!

Good listening is an active, not a passive activity. To listen well you must not only hear with your ears, but also with your eyes, your mind and your heart. You must sort and store that which you hear. You must decide what to discard and what to purposely forget. You must make judgments that take you from the realm of an adolescent to the realities of an adult. It should be done with great care.

This chapter started by asking, "Why?" There is one more reason, and sometimes there is no better way to say something than the way it has already been said. Why listen? To quote from a famous plaque which hangs in an office of the U.S. Senate:

"You ain't learnin' nothin' while you're talkin'."

# Chapter Sixteen

## The Hard Of Hearing

### How To Make Those Conversations Easier

Losing a large percentage of your hearing is perhaps one of the most difficult of all handicaps to live with for two reasons. First, it is the loneliest. People who are intelligent and have been active and involved all their lives, realize that ideas and information are flowing past them, but they are cut off, many times, from making any contribution. They have no alternative but to interrupt unless someone is thoughtful enough to include them in the conversation. Then, for reasons it is hard to understand, most people have little or no patience with this infirmity. Those who would go out of their way to help the blind, and would take all the time necessary to aid the cripple, will simply dismiss the isolation of an almost silent world with a pert and impatient "Skip it," or, "Never mind." They seem unaware that they, too, may well be afflicted in future years with at least a partial hearing infirmity.

In an interview given by Helen Keller, she was asked if she could have just one of her senses restored, which one would she ask for? Her answer was, "Oh, to hear!"

### Don't Shout

If someone in your home or office has difficulty hearing, and especially if it is an older person, try to resist the temptation to shout. Shouting is hard on you, often annoying to the listener and usually of very little value. As a general rule, the first tones that are lost are the ones in the higher frequencies of pitch. That is why you may find that your elderly relative hears your husband's voice more easily than yours; his tones are deeper. When women begin to yell, their throat muscles grow tighter and their voices become shrill, driving their voice into even higher pitches, and thereby further defeating their purpose. Think DOWN. Lower your tone, but not your volume, and ask again with careful articulation, "Janet, would you like tea or coffee?" This time she will find it easier to understand you.

## I Can Hear Better With My Glasses On

It may sound strange to you, at first, to hear someone say at the start of a conversation, "Wait a moment until I put my glasses on. I can always hear better when I'm wearing my glasses." No, she is not rattled, she can. The reason is that she can more clearly watch your expressions and see your articulation. It becomes especially arduous to follow anyone with lazy speech habits. Make an effort to look directly at the person with whom you are speaking, so that she can see you full-faced and then be sure to use your tongue, lips and jaw to articulate clearly. Don't over-exaggerate, as that will distort your expressions.

## The Hardest Words To Hear

Science, in its great strides ever forward, may have changed its mind about this fact since the days of the early 50's, when college students sat in Speech Therapy classes knitting argyle socks. But, in those "olden" days they were always told that the most difficult word in the English language to hear was "strawberry." Phonetically, it seems that "seal" is a better candidate, but those whose business it is to make these discoveries insist that it is "strawberry." Strawberry is followed by a long list of words, all incorporating the highest frequency sounds, made even more difficult to hear when spoken quickly and in a taut voice. (Should anyone ask you, or if you are looking for a good question as a conversation starter, you might like to know that the most phonetically beautiful word in our language is "home.")

Would you care to guess the word most easily heard and understood? Don't give up too quickly. Think a minute and you will probably come up with it. It is your own name. Notice how often you can be in a room filled with people, all talking, and you are paying strict attention to those in your group. Suddenly, someone across the room says your name in her conversational voice. You'll probably hear it. You may not hear what is said before or after it, but your name will ring out loud and clear, like a call from the Almighty.

Since this is true for all be sure to make it a point when addressing a person with a hearing disability to call her by name before you begin to say anything else. It is the quickest way to gain her attention. Face her squarely — start with her name and use all of the articulation skills you have been practicing, and most important of all, always, always take time to include her with understanding.

We are told that the young people who subject themselves for long hours to the thundering volume of today's popular music will lose some of their hearing sense at an earlier age than their parents. Most people find there is at least a slight adjustment in their hearing ability over a period of years. From time to time, it is wise to check, with a few simple questions, to test yourself on this point.

1. Do you find you do not identify familiar voices on the telephone or the television or in the next room as quickly as you used to? Is it more and more necessary to see, or to ask, "who is there"?
2. Are you aware of friends mentioning, occasionally, that you are speaking too loudly or too softly? Have they inferred lately that you seem to be speaking in a monotone now?
3. Can you hear a complete phone number and repeat it or jot it down correctly when it has been given to you only once? If you cannot, it may not be your memory failing, but only that you have confused the sound of two of the digits.
4. At cocktail parties, or in crowded rooms, do you find yourself leaning toward the person, not necessarily out of interest, but in order to hear her speak?
5. Do you find you must look at someone to hear him well? Do you realize that you hear better when you are wearing your glasses?
6. Do others mention noises that you did not hear? (A squeaking noise in your car, a pan steaming on the stove, a bird singing or a cat suddenly hissing?)

If you suspect you may have even a slight hearing impairment, it is important to have it checked. So much can be done to aid hearing now that was not known a generation ago. If a competent doctor tells you that nothing can be done at this time to improve your condition, just realizing and being alert to the trouble is in itself an advantage. You can often help yourself by keeping your eyes on the person to whom you are speaking and asking her to repeat when you are not sure you heard accurately what was said. If you are at a party or there is a distracting noise near you, lead the person to a quiet corner of the room so that you may better concentrate on the conversation. She will be flattered by your attention. Be quick to inform others that you have a little trouble hearing under certain conditions and ask them to speak a bit more slowly in order that you may grasp all that is said. Never simply withdraw if you find you have a hearing problem. Make every effort to follow all that is said and insist on co-operation.

If your hearing is perfect, be alert to the problems of others. Include everyone in your conversations and the extra effort you make to share with those who need your thoughtfulness will be deeply appreciated.

# Chapter Seventeen

## A "Poker Voice" I Suppose Is Good For Poker

### Rid Yourself Of A Monotone

If it turns out to be true that a "poker voice" is good for poker, I'm pretty sure you will find that's all it is good for. It is certainly never going to impress anyone that you have the sterling qualities of enthusiasm, leadership and persuasive abilities. The best thing to do with a monotone is to head for the big poker stakes in Las Vegas — or get rid of it. If you elect the second course of action, it's a surer bet.

Feminists might say it is from so many generations of fitting into a mold of conformity that so many women speak within a very narrow range. Language scientists might attribute it to our rapid rate of speech. Whatever the reason, it is time for women to take the lead — to speak up, speak out and speak with determination, directly and dramatically.

If you feel strongly about a matter it is pretty hard to relay that concern if you orchestrate the whole program on one note. Not only should your options be flexible today, but your voice should also be an adaptable and reinforcing partner in saying; "This I am — This I think — This I am aiming for — This I can accomplish — This I believe in — This is my faith."

Try reading those last short phrases out loud. How positive do you sound? Did your voice slam down like a fist on a podium? Did your tone say the matter was settled, or did it sound more as if you were waiting for someone to correct you or give you permission to feel that way? Try it again. Bang your fist down every time you say the word 'this'. Really bang it. Can you make your audience listen and believe? Does your voice need color? Not loudness, color. Here is the easiest way to develop it.

Somewhere on the bookshelf, or put away with your college texts, is a book of poetry. It's time to recycle it. Nothing will help you more than reading poetry out loud and recording it on tape for instant playback. Almost every word says to you, "Color me with my meaning." Make it powerful, lovely, singing, laughing, frightened, or sleepy by the way you say it. Almost any poems that are favorites of yours will do. Selected here are three among the thousands because each one has something so definite to offer your voice. Your goal in life is probably not to be a second Bette Davis, but you, too, are on stage and have an audience. Be your best. The easiest way to overcome a fault is to go to the other extreme, and this is just between you and your tape recorder. Make it a rousing session.

This first American classic, OH CAPTAIN, MY CAPTAIN, by Walt Whitman was written in honor of Abraham Lincoln. Whitman is comparing Lincoln to the captain of a ship (the ship of state) which is now returning from a battle (the Civil War) victorious. The people on shore are still cheering, not as yet having heard that their captain has been wounded and is dying. The voice must show strength and determination as well as sorrow and respect for the fallen leader.

You must read out loud now, even if you do not have a

tape recorder. Thinking through the expression will not help. It must be oral. It must, also, be done rather slowly. You can almost hear a cadence of drum beats in parts. The diagram lines will help you in accenting and pausing for expression.

Oh *Captain!*/*My* Captain! / our *fearful* trip is *done* /
The *ship* has *weathered* every *rack,* / the *prize* we *sought* is *won.* /
The *port* is near, / the *bells* I hear, / the *people* all exulting, /
While *follow* eye / the *steady* keel, / the *vessel* grim and *daring;* /
But oh *heart!* / *heart!* / *heart!* /
Oh the *bleeding* drops of red, /
Where on the deck my *Captain* lies, /
*Fallen* / *cold* and *dead.* /
*Exult* oh *shores* / and *ring* oh *bells!* /
But *I,* / with *mournful tread,* /
*Walk* the *deck* my *Captain* lies, /
*Fallen* / *cold* and *dead.* /

Oh *Captain!* / *My* Captain! / *rise up* and *hear* the bells; /
*Rise up* — / for *you* the *flag* is *flung* — for *you* the *bugle* trills; /
For *you* bouquets and ribboned *wreaths* — /
for *you* the shores are *acrowding,* /
For *you* they call, / the *swaying* mass, / their *eager faces* turning; /
*Here Captain!* / *dear father!* /
This *arm* beneath your *head!* /
It *is* some *dream* that on the deck
You've *fallen* / *cold* and *dead.* /

Columbus, By Joaquin Miller, moves along telling a

128

story with a wide variety of emotions. It is most dramatic. Make your voice paint the picture line by line. One line depends entirely upon the shading it is given to deliver its message and it was for this line that the poem was selected as an exercise for you. When you read, "A light, A light, A light, A light," it can sound almost imbecilic or it can express four completely different meanings as the author intended. It should be read so that it says, A light (Could that be a light?), A light (Yes, it is a light!), A light (Everyone look! We're saved, a light.), A light (Thank God — He's with us, a light.) It is not easy. Work with it for a while.

> *Behind* him / lay the *gray* Azores, /
> *Behind* / the *Gates* of *Hercules;* /
> *Before* him, / not a *ghost* of *shores,* /
> Before him, / only *shoreless* seas. /
> The good mate said: / *"Now* we must *pray,* /
> For lo / the very *stars* have gone, /
> *Brave* Admiral speak, / what *shall* I say?" /
> "Why *say,* / *Sail on,* / *sail on* and *on."* /

> "My *men* grow *mutinous* day by day; /
> My *men* grow *ghastly,* / *wan* and *weak."* /
> The *stout* mate thought of *home,* / a *spray*
> Of salt *wave washed* his *swarthy* cheek. /
> *"What* shall I *say,* / brave *Admiral* say, /
> If we sight *not* but *seas* at *dawn?"* /
> "Why *you* shall *say* at *break* of *day,* /
> Sail on — / sail on, / sail on and *on!"* /

Does your voice sound as though it could command mutinous men, or would you be having trouble getting the brownie troupe in line?

> Then, *pale* and *wan* he kept his deck, /
> And *peered* through *darkness.* / *Ah,* / *that* night

> Of *all dark* nights! / And *then* a speck — /
> A *light!* / A *light!* / A *light!* / A *light!* /
> It *grew,* / a *starlit* flag *unfurled,* /
> It *grew* to be *time's* burst of *dawn.* /
> He *gained* a *world;* / he *gave* that *world*
> Its *grandest* lesson: / "*Oh,* / sail *on!*" /

Take a break from the drama for a minute. For a lighter and completely different feeling, try this little jingle. Realize the difference in both its tone and its pace. Have fun with it. Put a smile in your voice and listen for it as you read.

> Said a *very* small *wren* /
> To a *very* large *hen,* /
> "Pray? / *Why* do you *make* such a *clatter?*" /
> "I *never* could guess /
> Why an *egg* / more or less /
> Should be *thought* so *important* a *matter.*" /

By now you are probably thinking that Dustin Hoffman and Sally Field are never going to be in danger of losing center stage to you. That's all right. Your aim is not to be the next Oscar winner, but you do want to convey to the next committee meeting that you can say what you mean, and that you mean what you say, and it would be best if they paid attention. Keep in mind that is exactly what you are working on and this will help.

Now, are you ready for the big ones? Few can equal Edgar Allan Poe in his use of onomatopoeia, words that take the sound of their meaning. It is absolutely essential, when you read aloud The Bells, that your voice carries the sound of each of the different sets of bells. It is not easy, but it is an excellent discipline. Many lines have been omitted from this poem, as they have from the others, so as not to discourage anyone from trying, but you might like to look up the complete selections for your own benefit as you feel you progress. Try taking your voice down one step at a time as you repeat:

bells
  bells
    bells
      bells
        bells
          bells
            bells

Hear the sleds with the bells — Silver bells —
What a world of merriment their melody foretells!
How they tinkle, tinkle, tinkle,
In the icy air of night!
While the stars that oversprinkle
All the heavens, seem to twinkle
With a crystalline delight;
Keeping time, time, time
In a Rantco of Runic rhyme,
To the tintinnabulation that so musically wells
From the bells, bells, bells, bells,
   bells, bells, bells —
From the jingling and the tinkling of the bells.

Hear the mellow wedding bells — Golden bells!
What a world of happiness their harmony foretells!
Through the balmy air of night
How they ring out their delight —
From the molten-golden notes,
And all in tune.

Hear the tolling of the bells — Iron bells
What a world of solemn thought their monody compels!
In the silence of the night,
How we shiver with affright
At the melancholy menace of their tone!

For every sound that floats
From the rust within their throats
Is a groan.

Now, let's inject some of that color and forcefulness into these thoughts. Again, say them out loud, into your recorder and listen objectively and ask yourself if you were listening to someone else, if you would be convinced.

I am not "just" a woman; I am a confident woman, a concerned woman, a sympathetic woman, a well-informed woman, a loving woman, a woman of faith. I am a total woman. I can achieve all that I dream.

You can, you know.

Then SAY IT! COME ON — *SAY IT!*

To explore the wide range of meanings you control by your inflections, take a simple phrase and see how many different ways you can say it to completely change its meaning. Start with the three words, "I love you." Repeat them out loud now, saying them to:

- a child who has just done something endearing;
- a friend who has cheered you up and made you laugh;
- your sister who has received bad news and feels completely alone and deserted;
- a stray puppy you just brought home and he's crying;
- a dear relative who knows she is soon to die;
- signing off a telephone conversation with your husband;
- congratulating your son upon his college graduation.

How many other meanings can you add to this list?

Count the number of meanings you can put into the words, "Good-morning" or "Hello" and "not really."

Much is said, especially in the news media, about statements or phrases that are taken out of context, but it is never questioned if the expression has been misinterpreted. It might be purposeful, the next time someone tells you that a friend or co-worker said something which on the surface sounds untrue, uncharitable or exaggerated, to ask, "But, how did she say it?"

# Chapter Eighteen

## How To Handle Embarrassing Mistakes

"I thought I'd die! I absolutely thought I'd die."

Those were the first words she spoke when she faced the Effective Speaking class. Embarrassment still was apparent in her manner.

It seems she had been asked to accept an office in a social organization. She was not told that one of the duties was to introduce their immediate past president at the annual meeting. She had never faced an audience before. She made giant cue cards and wrote every word in big, bold letters. She depended on them to do the job.

She thought she started off pretty well. She made it to the speaker's stand and when she opened her mouth, she was pleased to hear her voice was still there. She read the first card and looked down for the second one — it wasn't there! None of the remaining cards were there. She had no idea where she had left them! A feeling of stark panic rushed over her! The first card ended with the words, "We are grateful to our former president for all the events she undertook last year" — the list of events was written on the next card — the missing card! Terror swallowed her! Her mind went completely blank; she couldn't think of a single former event. She repeated the last sentence again in a desperate play for time, hoping for a miracle. None came. She knew the list was long, but she couldn't remember any of it. Repeating the last line for the third time, she could not at that moment even remember the Christmas party, much less an entire ten months of innovative programs. She was certain of only one thing — she needed some help in Public Speaking. She knew there had to be a way to handle this embarrassment, she just didn't know what it was.

If you stop and think for a minute, can you recall the most embarrassing thing that ever happened to you? How about the worst mistake you ever made? Those things are pretty hard to forget. Ask a group of people those two questions, and you will see every head nod "yes." Embarrassing mistakes are very much like aches and pains; they are mostly of great importance only to the person who suffers them. Every person must find her own way of dealing with them, and given enough time, everyone will have some whoppers!

Basically, there are only three prescriptions that are potent remedies for such stressful situations.

### Can You Correct It?

If it is a slip of the tongue, and it needs correction, correct it immediately and without fanfare. The more flustered you become, the more you enlarge it. If you can't erase it, at least allow it to be as minimal as possible. Cope with it. If it calls for an apology, give it at once — and only once, but directly and sincerely. You may have to swallow hard, but if it's your fault, own up to it. Your tone of voice is important. Keep it low. If an apology is twittered out amid embarrassed giggles, it is more apt to compound the error than relieve it. Omit the temptation to say a string of self-belittling remarks like, "Wasn't that dumb of me? I don't know why I always say the wrong thing! I am so embarrassed etc., etc." It is best to restore the situation to normal as soon as possible, there is no good to be accomplished by prolonging it. If you are addressing a group of people, it may not be something you've said that causes the embarrassment, but something you know you should be saying and have completely forgotten.

Where help is available, reach for it. Even seasoned public speakers have been known to lose their train of thought, or draw a complete blank on a simple word. They will usually ask the audience to supply the term for them and continue right along without fanfare. You have no doubt seen that happen several times, but you did not dwell on it because the speaker did not make an issue of it. If you are not overly severe with yourself, others seldom will judge you more harshly. If a speaker finds she has momentarily forgotten her next point, she may ask if someone in the audience would take a minute to restate the ideas presented to that point. That minute or two of time, and the review of the material, will start her off again. (This would have been a solution for the lady with the missing cards; to suggest that those in the audience, the direct participants in the events, join with her in listing the outstanding meetings of the past year.)

Try always to be aware of times when you can help others over an uncomfortable situation. If you are close to a speaker and she has lost a word, don't just watch her struggle, supply it.

### Can You Find A Little Humor?

If you can laugh at yourself, you'll save many a tear. If you have only brought embarrassment down on yourself, there is already much to be grateful for. (Better by far that you fall up the stairs and rip your only designer gown, than that you trip your boss's wife and see her sitting on the floor in front of you!) You want to relieve your own, and everyone else's sympathetic awkwardness as quickly as possible. Speak up, with a smile and quick reassurance that all is well. There are very few situations which do not encompass some humor, if you look for it.

Have you ever sat with a group of friends when the conversation turned to blunders and unpredicted crises that had happened to them? Before long, you were probably laughing so hard your sides were aching. The more that was confessed, the funnier it became. Being able to laugh at yourself must be God's psychotherapy.

Perhaps you've watched TV programs where they run off throw-away tapes of horrendous mistakes made by the actors or stage crew. Everyone in the audience and usually the people who made the fluff, dissolves in laughter.

Many years ago a big name personality was receiving, on camera, a very expensive watch as an award. He not only thanked the company's biggest competitor by mistake, he also launched into a long recital about the merits of this competitor over all the other watch manufacturers. As quickly as they could manage it, they cut him off and ran a commercial. When he returned, he shook his head and simply said in a quiet, sincere tone, "You are looking at the man with the reddest face in television." He then immediately stated the name of the correct company, thanked them, and moved along. He has made amends to the company many times since with free TV exposure by telling the story as a huge joke on himself, and mentioning the donor and its excellence repeatedly. Fluffs are hilarious when other people make them, and they can really be just as funny when they happen to you. Your attitude, your speech, your tone of voice will make them so.

## Can You Forget It?

If you cannot correct or laugh — forget. Perhaps that is not the correct word, since it is impossible to consciously forget anything. Since we are dealing with speech, let us borrow a more succinct term and say it is best to "adopt a non-verbalization policy." This "non-verbalization policy" is to remain in effect until you can see the humorous side of the incident, or forever!

Some episodes can be avoided with just a little advance thought and precaution. Think through the upcoming event and predispose of as many pitfalls as possible. If you are to receive an award, will you have to climb stairs onto a stage? Make sure your gown will not trip you and practice lifting it at home. (Don't forget your slip. Many a woman has lifted her gown, only to trip on her slip.) You should also pick up this book again and review the chapters on Public Speaking to reassure yourself that your brief "thank you" speech will be impressive.

If you are to attend a social function, think ahead of the people whom you are most likely to meet there. Review names, and have a conversation starter in mind in case it is needed.

Take your time. Most accidents occur because someone is rushing, or attempting to do several things at the same time. Set your cocktail down before you stand to greet someone. Glance down to check for an unexpected step before entering an unfamiliar room. Don't be afraid to speak up and ask if someone's name slips your mind. It happens to everyone, thankfully, and others understand. Wear your glasses if you need them. They can be a most attractive accessory today. Know the number of cocktails you can have and stop well before that number. Do not confuse what you can "usually" consume with what you can "always" enjoy. When in doubt about the "correct" thing to do, remember that good manners are simply doing that which shows consideration and makes the other person comfortable. From time to time, pick up this book and check again the material that proves to be the most practical in your situation.

If you do all of this, and you still make a mistake, what then? Well, what then? You have perhaps found a weakness and you can go to work on correcting it. Tomorrow you will have improved. The only other thing you have done, is prove yourself to be just like the rest of us — human, and is that really so bad?

# Chapter Nineteen

## How To Disagree And Stay Friends

An old truism tells us that when two people agree on everything, one of them is unnecessary. The Polyanna Sunshine of past years who smiled at everyone and agreed with everything, by today's standards might well be considered an ineffectual woman and lacking in convictions. You don't want to sidestep every disagreement, but you do want to avoid becoming a disagreeable person. You have every right to speak out and speak up, but before you do you would be wise to answer two questions directed solely to yourself.

The first question with which you must come to grips is this: is the matter important? Everyone's life is filled with daily minor aggravations and annoyances. If you are constantly marching to battle, you soon lose all effectiveness. The woman who repeatedly complains about everything from the cold coffee to the slow traffic is "tuned out" by all who know her. Her voice becomes colorless, high and singsong, and she is labeled as a shrew, a crab and a nagger. No one pays attention to a chronic complainer. She is ignored or simply is tolerated if absolutely necessary. But the woman who on occasion points out a significant matter in a tone that says, "pay attention, there is an issue here we must settle" and proceeds with both her voice and her speech to arrive at a solution, commands not only attention, but respect.

The second question may be even more important than the first, and you must answer it clearly if you are to avoid frustration and a self-destructive anger. You must know what end result you want, and when you have reached it. If you are not sure where you want to go, you had better wait a bit before you start. Your voice, your speech, your manner, must all have direction, and what is satisfactory for one person may not be sufficient compensation for another. Consider the following story thoughtfully and take a minute or two, if necessary, to decide which of these two women you would identify with more closely.

A woman arrived at an Effective Speaking class one evening, excited and anxious to share an experience she had had with her classmates. The class had been discussing the values of self-control and the positive approach in voice and manner when faced with troublesome opposition in the office. She was eager to point out how well this system worked at home, too.

She and her husband had been invited to a 25th anniversary party being held for neighbors they were both fond of, and she was looking forward to a special evening. She had fixed one of her favorite casseroles for a potluck buffet and she was dressed and ready when her husband arrived home — storm warnings flying!

Everything had gone wrong all day. He was angry, tired, frustrated, upset, and not in any mood to go to that "stupid" party. As a matter of fact, he was *not* going. If she wanted to go, she could go by herself. She did want to go, but not by herself; that was not the picture she had been looking forward to all day.

In the past, she said she would have told him vehemently just what she thought of his juvenile attitude and selfish behavior, but she caught her breath and decided to work from an affirmative stand.

"I understand how you must feel," she said. "If I'd had a day like that I wouldn't want to go to a party either, and it might be better to skip it for tonight. I know they'll be disappointed, as they were especially looking forward to having you there, but later they'll understand. I'll just run over to the kitchen door now and drop off the casserole I made, and why don't you shower and have a drink and relax. When I come back, if you think you feel like going for a few minutes, we will, but you can decide later."

Off she went with her casserole and she took her time delivering it. When she returned, her husband had showered and changed and she sat down and talked with him on another matter. After a few preliminary remarks he said, "Well, I suppose we should go over to the party for a few minutes, but we'll just say hello and come right home."

"O.K." she agreed, "I know they'll be so pleased to see you."

They stayed the entire evening — they both had a great time, and she was delighted that her positive approach, and her control of the annoyance that usually showed in her voice, had worked and produced the exact result she wanted.

Most of the class listened and shared her pleasure, but when she finished, another woman said, "I have a question. When you came home that night, did you give the good boy some cookies and warm milk and tuck him into bed?"

Two completely different women, each with a different idea of a valuable conclusion. One wanted to win the peace, the other preferred total surrender in war. The woman who attended the party with her husband and had a great time achieved exactly what she wanted — the second woman, in her place, would have felt she had compromised, and that only by having her husband apologize and admit he had been inconsiderate of her, would her pride have been salvaged. The second woman admitted she would have been willing to forgo the party and have quite a row to reach that end, but then the air would have been cleared for her, and she would not have had a feeling of resentment festering inside of her.

There is seldom a clear right or wrong when it comes to feelings, but there is a crystal edit — "Know thyself." Before you speak, know where your speech is directed; do you want to change a course of action or do you want to definitely establish that there is a difference of opinion, and you are right. If you want one result and achieve the other, it can be a hollow victory, indeed. Your tone of voice and manner of speaking will follow the mental directions you issue.

It's also a wise person who knows when she has reached her goal. There are many ways of saying "I'm sorry" and if they are rejected because the other person doesn't understand that is what is being said, there may be unnecessary bitterness on both sides.

In another class a woman, well into her 60s, said, "I have something I want to share with all you younger ladies. I want to tell you how my husband of over 40 years apologizes to me."

"I learned very early in our marriage that it was impossible for him to say, 'I'm sorry — I was wrong.' I'd wait for days, and I knew by his actions that he was trying, but the words wouldn't come. Finally, I found a way to help him. I'd sit on the arm of his chair and say, 'You're very sorry, aren't you? You really know that was an inconsiderate thing for you to do, don't you?' He'd give a grunt and a nod of his head and the apology was made — and accepted. Over the years he has said some beautiful things; that he loved me dearly, never wanted to upset me, that he appreciated my worth in his life and that he felt real sorrow when he was unfair to me. He has also admitted that he was wrong, dead wrong at times. He has said it all in his heart, repeating it silently after me, and with his voice by a grunt and a nod of his head. You have to make an effort sometimes to understand, but that man is worth understanding!"

Many times the fine line between discussion and disagreement is crossed unnecessarily. Here are a few Do's and Don'ts you can use to direct and control your speech and avoid unnecessary confrontations.

### Don'ts

— Cross out the words "I told you so" from your vocabulary. File them away with all the other phrases you know, but with your standards, refuse to use. You can be sure that once a disaster has occurred, the other person remembers very well that you told her and never needs to be reminded again.

— It is seldom necessary to prove a person wrong beyond a doubt. Once your point has been accepted, don't belabor it. It is time now to move on.

— Avoid sarcasm as you would germ warfare. Remarks such as, "That's so stupid, it sounds just like you," accomplish nothing. A disagreement can be much like major surgery — when the operation is over and the trouble removed, an ugly scar can remain. The cutting edge of your voice and the belittling remarks in your speech are often clearly remembered long after the issue itself has been settled.

— Never correct or chastise in front of other employees, friends or even family members if it is at all possible to do it in private.

— If there is a difference of opinion, keep it limited to the people involved. To broadcast it is self-defeating and to ask others to take sides is totally unfair.
— Your words can prove dangerous — think well before you make any threat, and if you choose to threaten, be ready to stand behind it. A threat is effective only once, if it is not carried out.
— You need to keep your voice in control and refrain from shouting. (Chinese say the first one to shout loses the argument.) But never, never argue with silence. If your point isn't worth presenting, it isn't worth having.
— Don't belittle the person by referring to her limited education, lesser position, excess weight, or any type of mental or physical limitation.
— Never assume a dogmatic superiority or talk down to another person. A condescending tone can be more obnoxious than a screaming voice.
— Never, never laugh when someone presents a theory that is a serious matter to her.
— Avoid all generalizations. It has never been proven that much has been said, thought or done by "*all* you men" — "*all* young kids" or "*every* blessed dog owner in the state!"
— Never award nicknames. It is a sure sign of insecurity, and always detracts from your personal image.

### Do's

— Let the other person finish whatever it is she wants to say. You may have heard it before (many times) and you may know exactly what is coming, but let her say it again, without interruption.
— Give a verbal "hand up" when you've won your

point. Good sportsmanship on the playing field is recognized and appreciated when an opponent offers a hand to help the person up whom he has knocked down. Your thoughtful statement to reestablish a person's pride immediately, shows the same fine caliber of fairness.

— When possible, suggest, rather than demand. A "don't you think a bright yellow paint will attract more attention than a pale green one?" rates higher marks in diplomacy than "you know darn well no one ever is attracted to a sick green anything."

— Be sure you understand exactly what is being said. You may have heard someone disagree strongly with something said by a third party and realized at once that they were both talking about different things. One person had heard the other's meaning incorrectly. It is not an uncommon situation and is easily caught with a single precaution. The safest thing to do is to always start by asking, "Do I understand correctly that what you are saying is" or "what you are asking me to do is" or "that the way you feel about this is". The other party may then respond with, "No, my point was not" and the confrontation may well be avoided.

— It is wise whenever possible to choose a special time to discuss matters which may be upsetting. The end of the day is seldom the most advantageous time to approach a problem. Some issues must be faced at once, pleasant or not, but if you have the option of choosing a time, try the mornings or right after lunch.

— Keep in mind at all times the importance of your tone of voice. If you speak in quiet, controlled tones you can often calm down the most excitable person. If you feel your voice tightening and your emotions getting out of hand, postpone the matter until another time. Your voice, held in its lower ranges, will say, "Let's talk this over," not "We'll thrash this out *right now.*"

— Go from your opponent's point of view to yours. If you start by saying, "I appreciate your point of view," or "I understand how you feel," it softens your dictate with a touch of sympathy. (Remember Mary Poppins' "spoonful of sugar that helps the medicine go down?" It does, you know.)

— When pointing out a weakness or a fault, it is wise to start with a praiseworthy point first. "I am impressed with the thoroughness of your report, but I feel we must make some adjustments in the number of days you are allowing for this project" is a better beginning than, "there is no way we are going to sit still and allow the length of time you are demanding to do this job."

— Always suggest a correction or a solution when you point out an error.

— There are three sentences that cannot be said by a small, petty minded person: I'm sorry, I was wrong, and excuse me please. It takes a superior person to admit she is wrong — and isn't that the kind of person you want to be?

— Most important of all — develop good speech and a poor memory. When the difficulty has been resolved, forget it. If you have achieved your goal, let the matter rest. If you didn't gain all that you wished, forget that, too, and move on. It is not always the easy thing to do, but it is the wisest and most productive.

One lingering question may remain. You understand the framework of a productive discussion, but the other person doesn't. It takes two, and one, perhaps, wouldn't read anything constructive even if it were handed to her. Is there then any point in abiding by the guidelines alone?

Yes, there are four important gains for you. First, even if you do not achieve your end, you are sure that there was nothing more you could have said or have done to present your argument in a better light. You have accomplished all that was possible. Second, you did not necessarily lose any ground. Third, you kept your emotions under control and did not hurt anyone, thereby preventing future regrets and fourth, and most important of all — win or lose, isn't it a nice feeling to know that you're a lady!

# Chapter Twenty

## We'd Like To Interview You On TV

It is possible, but highly unlikely, that you will make it through this life without ever being asked to publicly express your opinion on some matter, or share your expertise with a radio or TV audience. Even though you are sitting there now thinking, "NO — NEVER — I WOULDN'T!!", you may still find yourself someday behind a mike and the cameras grinding away. It may be simply a public opinion poll, or a reporter asking a few questions because you were right where the action was. Even if it amounts to only a few brief seconds, you will want to appear composed and knowledgeable when thousands of people are later listening to your answers. More likely your company, your church, your favorite charity or some activity in which you have been involved will necessitate your arriving at a studio ready to talk for some minutes on a subject with which you are very familiar. Don't panic — there are no known fatalities! If you are completely honest with yourself you may even admit later that it was fun.

First of all, remember that as in the case of giving a speech, no one is going to ask you to speak on a subject that you know nothing about. If someone else were more qualified, or capable of making a better presentation, she would have been asked instead of you, so begin by relaxing and savoring the compliment. You'll be great!

Then place your faith in the people you'll be working with. They are all professionals, they know how to obtain the best results and they are dedicated to making their program the most stimulating production aired in that time slot. A big part of that consists of making *you* look good. Never, never will they intimidate you, belittle you or attempt to make you ill at ease. Co-operation is the hallmark of a professional. (This chapter does not relate to programs dealing with controversial issues. If you have just agreed to appear on 60 Minutes you may need an immediate crash course in composure.)

In addition to the aid you will receive from all station personnel, there are some preparations you can make to help yourself and assist those in charge.

For both radio and TV programs plan your time so that you can arrive quite early, and have a chance to become familiar and comfortable with the different surroundings. If you are going to a TV studio, be sure you know ahead if you are expected to bring any visual aids such as tapes, slides, displays or charts. Make sure they are brought to the Program Director as soon as you arrive, and do not shorten this poor person's life by allowing him to plan a video section around material that you didn't have the time to pick up, or changed your mind about. (Professionals have nerves, too — honest!)

Make it as easy for your interviewer as possible. Think a bit about the most important facts that you want to bring out beforehand. (You are the authority on this subject.) Write questions down and submit them, and then allow the person in charge to select the ones he feels will make the most interesting conversation. Be sure to answer the questions with something a bit more lively than "yes" or "no," and never "yup," "nope" or nod. It is not necessary to go on forever, like the boy on the burning deck, or an opera singer dying on stage. If you pay attention to your host you will soon realize the pace the producers are trying to set.

Bob Chadburn, a fine area news man, tells about the time he was to interview a national politician and the gentleman asked him how long Bob wanted him to speak. "If your explanation would run about a minute, sir, that would be just fine," Bob said.

"A minute!" bellowed the politician — "Great guns, the only time I ever did anything that fast before a camera was when I waved to my mother."

The "paying attention" suggestion really deserves capitals, for unless there is something you wish to address to the audience in general (in which case you look directly into the camera with the little red light) you should direct your remarks to the person with whom you are speaking. Absolutely nothing comes across more amateurish than someone trying to sneak a look at herself in the monitor (the screen on the set for checking purposes). Forget completely that it's even there. It cannot be said too many times, or in too many situations, to always be thoroughly familiar with your material, but do not try to memorize it. If you have dates or figures that you wish to include it will make you a bit more comfortable to jot them down and keep them inconspicuously in your hand — glancing down to reaffirm them in your mind when you are sure the camera is not right on you. Remember, too, that you do not need to raise your voice as you might in other public speaking situations, as microphones today are extremely sensitive, but good diction and clear articulation are as important as ever.

Of course, you will want to look your best. If your hair is neat and off your face, and your outfit appropriate for the program (you are always safe with a basic dress, never overdone with ruffles or excessive sparkling jewelry) you will be more at ease and better able to concentrate on immediate matters. Once you have arrived at the station, the best thing to do about your appearance is to check it once and then forget about it. The exception to that is to be aware of your facial expressions and posture. Many people, when sincerely interested in a subject and concentrating, tend to frown. It often comes across as an unfriendly scowl or a critical attitude. If you start with a smile it will do much to erase those lines from your face.

Be sure in your effort to appear assured and comfortable that you do not slump down in your chair. If you remember to sit up straight, not only will you sound better but you will photograph pounds slimmer! BE AWARE OF YOUR LEGS. Be sure when you seat yourself that your knees are together and if you cross your legs that it is at the ankles and never at the knees. Women have been wearing pants suits for so long that they now find with today's trend back to dresses they must adjust their habits to the newer styles. You might take a minute at home, in the outfit you will be wearing, to find a comfortable position and check it out in your full length mirror. If you are not using your hands to demonstrate or gesture, simply allow them to rest gracefully in your lap. Avoid any temptation to play with jewelry, fix your hair or put your hands to your face. Fidgeting or tight fisted hands are always a tell-tale sign of nervousness, so keep your hands relaxed and quiet.

Behind a camera or a microphone, courtesy and consideration for the comfort of others is just as important as it is in a business conference and just as appreciated.

Make it a point to listen to or view the program on which you will be appearing as many times as possible before your guest date. It will enable you to become familiar with the people you'll be with and help you to understand what they are looking for in their format.

Humor, in good taste, is always appreciated if it can be worked in comfortably, but if it is not your forte it is much better omitted than sent off to die on the airwaves.

When you are watching guests on the preceding programs, observe them objectively. How do they sit, stand and move, and how do they differ from the professionals? Are they projecting a pleasant, relaxed image? How? Is their message coming across? What makes it so effective? What can you learn from watching them? Do they seem to be having a good time? You will too.

Now, when the phone rings and a cheery voice says, "We'd like to have you come over to our studio and be a guest on our talk show," say "Great! Let me jot down the date and time and I'll be there." Sure you can — just be yourself and enjoy!

# Chapter Twenty-One

## Just Between Us

Dear Readers,

We've done a great deal of talking about "showcasing" you. Will this make you someone you are not? Never. Will it make you a leader in spite of a lack of determination? Impossible. If you follow every single suggestion will you become Ms. Popularity of the '80s? I'm afraid not. How about combining this with a "How to Dress" book? Instant success? Not if that is all you have — just the appearance.

In the long run you will be recognized, liked, even loved for your own individual character. Basically, enduring popularity and respect are not something you can easily contrive to obtain, nor scheme to gain by employing any number of subterfuges.

You have often heard it said that this person or that person "grows on you," or "wears well." You will ultimately be judged on your character, your sincere concern for others, your capabilities, your flexibility, your attitude and your moral principles. The most silver-tongued perfectionist may make a gargantuan first impression, but she will never hold it if she hasn't the fundamentals which make a truly worthwhile person.

No book was ever written on popularity, speech, fashion, make-up or "how to" that is capable of putting depth into shallowness. What it can do is point out to you the proven, successful ways of aiding others to see in you, more quickly, the qualities and qualifications you have to offer. It can encourage you to strive for ever more worthwhile goals and remind you again and again, that when you stop trying to improve, you stop being good.

If you are really on the move and conscientiously trying to advance, be very sure that you don't now overlook the area which will ultimately determine how far you will progress and how quickly you will meet your goals.

Do you feel you still have a long way to go? We all do. But as President Kennedy, and others before him said, we start with a single step. Never forget, you must then keep going! The glory is not in the step but in the start.

Do not try to do too much at once. Follow the steps which are suggested in the initial personal quiz and re-read the introduction. (You didn't read the introduction? Shame on you! Go back and read it now. It has something important to say to you.)

Promise yourself that you will start today — not tomorrow — today, NOW! Consciously look for those characteristics which make other people respected and leaders, and systematically develop in yourself your potential for effectiveness.

I wish I could take credit for these words with which I have chosen to close. But I cannot. I do not know who wrote them. Rather, I can invite you to join with me in striving to live each day by them.

> Do more than exist . . . live,
> Do more than look . . . observe,
> Do more than read . . . absorb,
> Do more than hear . . . listen,
> Do more than think . . . ponder,
> Do more than plan . . . act,
> Do more than talk . . . say something,
>     (and then — say it well!)